Psychic Empath Warrior

A Survival Guide for Sensitive Empaths to Understand and Improve the Development of Their Psychic and Empathetic Abilities and Protect from Narcissists and Energy Vampires

Diana Ortega

© **Copyright 2019 - All rights reserved.**

The content contained within this book may not be reproduced, duplicated or transmitted without direct written permission from the author or the publisher.

Under no circumstances will any blame or legal responsibility be held against the publisher, or author, for any damages, reparation, or monetary loss due to the information contained within this book, either directly or indirectly.

Legal Notice:

This book is copyright protected. It is only for personal use. You cannot amend, distribute, sell, use, quote or paraphrase any part, or the content within this book, without the consent of the author or publisher.

Disclaimer Notice:

Please note the information contained within this document is for educational and entertainment purposes only. All effort has been executed to present accurate, up to date, reliable, complete information. No warranties of any kind are declared or implied. Readers acknowledge that the author is not engaging in the rendering of legal, financial, medical or professional advice. The content within this book has been derived from various sources. Please consult a licensed professional before attempting any techniques outlined in this book.

By reading this document, the reader agrees that under no circumstances is the author responsible for any losses, direct or indirect, that are incurred as a result of the use of information contained within this document, including, but not limited to, errors, omissions, or inaccuracies.

Table of Contents

Introduction 7
Chapter 1: Are You A Psychic Empath? 10
    Qualities of a Psychic Empath 10
    Struggles of an Empath 17
Chapter 2: Types of Psychic Empaths 24
Chapter 3: Key Enemies of an Empath 28
    The Melodramatic Vampire 29
    The Victim Vampire 31
    The Narcissist Vampire 32
    The Intimidator Vampire 35
    Judgmental Vampire 36
    The Innocent or Unknowing Vampire 38
Signs of Emotional Exhaustion 39
Chapter 4: Thriving as a Psychic Empath 47
Chapter 5: Long-Term Survival Strategies 54
Chapter 6: Owning Your Superpowers 66
    Top Superpowers of Every Psychic Empath 66
    Using Your Superpowers to Impact the World 71
    Mistakes Stopping You from Exploring Your Superpowers 79
    Fine Tuning Your Psychic Abilities 84
Chapter 7: Common Myths That Psychic Empaths

Should Never Believe *93*
Conclusion *102*

Introduction

In psychology, empathy is a key component of being emotionally intelligent. In a world that is starting to appreciate emotional intelligence over the more traditional intelligence that is book smart, empathy counts as the main ingredient for improved social interactions. Empathy is defined in dictionaries and by psychologists as: the ability to understand and share in the thoughts and emotions of another person. In other terms, empathy entails putting yourself in another person's shoes so that you can understand where they are coming from and how they feel. It involves seeing the world from the perspective of another person so that you can appreciate their world, fears, struggles, and even joys much better.

Empathy is not the same thing as sympathy, even though most people will use the two terms interchangeably to refer to the same thing. While sympathy is mainly just pity, empathy involves going the extra step of trying to find a solution for someone's suffering. Sympathy says, "Oh, that's terrible, I feel so sorry for her" and then walks away, while empathy stays a bit longer in hopes that they can alleviate the pain at hand. Most human beings are born with the capacity to be empathetic. However, the extent to which this capacity is explored depends on the kind of nurturing that a person receives as they grow up.

So far, empathy does sound like a good thing. In fact, the world would be a better place if all of us were empathetic towards each other. There would be less judgment and less resentment. The world would be friendlier and a safe place where people's feelings and thoughts would be given equal priority, and nobody would feel unseen or unheard. Unfortunately, we do not live in an idealistic world where everything is perfect and flawless. We live among people who are capable of empathy, and also among others who consider empathy a weak concept. There is still another category of people who are completely incapable of being empathetic.

In our day to day lives, we demonstrate the ability to be empathetic towards others when we set aside time and energy to commiserate with their suffering. Even when we are best-intentioned, there are instances when we might not act in ways that are empathetic towards others. Other times, we might only feel some sympathy and then move along. This brings us to a slightly different category of people who demonstrate a more advanced form of empathy. These people are known as empaths.

An empath differs from an empathetic person in this way: while empathetic people are able to relate with other people's thoughts and emotions, empaths actually feel these emotions and thoughts as though they were their own. An empathetic person might relate to the pain of a colleague and then go on with their life. An empath will usually wallow in this pain because they feel it as if it is their own. A psychic empath is able to pick up another person's pain without necessarily being told. Their psychic ability allows them to tune into the suffering of another person even when this may not be so obvious to those who rely on verbal and visual cues.

There are different reasons why some people are empaths, while others only seem to experience moments when they are empathetic towards others. Nature is the first culprit in churning empaths. Some people are born with heightened sensitivity. You can see it in the way they respond to things, even when they are still small babies. They seem more alert and more attuned to their surroundings. The kind of nurturing that a person receives while they are growing up can also impact their development into an adult empath. If your sensitivity is honored for the gift that it is, you will likely grow up in the full glory of your empath self. On the other hand, experiencing trauma as a child has been shown to hinder a person's empathic abilities. Think of it this way —a child that is brought up in a caring and loving household has a better chance of becoming a caring and loving adult when she grows up.

If you are a psychic empath, you might have a very hard time going through the day since you are constantly surrounded by all this pain and suffering that you are aware of. It is important to learn how to shield yourself from emotional, mental, and physical drain while at the same time helping those who need your help. However, you must learn how to tell the difference between those who genuinely need your help and those who are only trying to take advantage of you.

In this book, you will learn everything you need to know to go from being a psychic empath to being a psychic empath *warrior*. A psychic empath warrior is one who harnesses their power to do good, instead of simply being at the mercy of their abilities and the energy of those around them. As a psychic warrior, you will have greater control over your emotions, and you will not go through life feeling overwhelmed and drained. You will learn to recognize the qualities that set you apart from the average person, how to identify energy vampires, and how to protect yourself from situations that will drain your energy. If you have always struggled to understand why you feel things the way you do, this book will act as a handbook that will make everything clearer.

The main objective of this book is to help you realize that what you have is a great gift that you can use to positively impacting the world and others while also taking good care of yourself.

Chapter 1: Are You A Psychic Empath?

Are you a psychic empath or are you just an empathetic person? Sometimes the line between these two can be blurry. Even the person who struggles with empathy sometimes has days when they really seem to feel other people's pain. This could be circumstantial. For instance, you are likely to feel more empathetic towards someone who is closer to you than a person you've just met. You may also extend empathy more easily if you've been through the same situation in the past. That being said, an empath definitely has qualities that stand out in relation to the way they share in other people's feelings of pain.

Unlike the average empathetic person who has their off days where they don't seem to care about anybody else but themselves, psychic empaths hardly have any downtime. They feel and sense energy right from the moment they wake up to the time they go to bed unless they know how to shield themselves.

There are some greatly distinguishing characteristics that set apart the psychic empath. These are elaborated in the section below:

Qualities of a Psychic Empath

You are aware of everything around and in you

The average person is often aware of what is going on in their life, at least to a reasonable extent. They can tell what they are thinking about, they are peripherally aware of what is happening in their external environment, and they are able to read the verbal and visual cues from the people they are surrounded by. A psychic empath takes this a notch higher. They can sense just about everything in themselves and their external environment. They are able to walk in a room and immediately read the mood of the room. They can tell when a person is getting angry or upset even before it shows on their face. If you are a psychic empath, you will find yourself being very aware of what is happening in your life and even in the lives of the people you care about. If a friend is going through a heartbreak, you will share their pain in a way that others cannot, even before your friend makes this pain public knowledge.

You hate crowds and prefer being alone

While you care a lot about people, you also prefer to interact with them on a one-on-one basis and not while they are in a crowd. You find crowds overwhelming and prefer to keep your own company. You like solitude because it allows you to recharge your energy. You cannot survive for long in a crowd setting. Crowds steal your joy; they make you nervous and anxious and they drain you. The reason why crowds drain you so easily is because you are constantly picking up energy signals from people and being in a crowd means you are bombarded with so many signals that you get overwhelmed. Do you prefer staying indoors to going out? Are you the kind of person who would rather watch a concert on TV than actually attend the concert in person?

You are an amazing listener

A downside of being known as a good listener is that people tend to take that as their cue to dump all their problems on you. If you have been suspecting all along that you are an empath, this is a problem that you likely have. Empaths are often keen to truly understand people and they do this by listening more than they talk. People love good listeners. Most people love talking about themselves and will gravitate towards anyone who gives them the chance. Because of your good listening abilities, you may have found yourself playing therapist to friends and strangers alike. Unfortunately for you, you might not have a whole lot of empaths in your life who return the favor. The journal you write in every night before you go to bed might be the only listening ear that you turn to after you have spent your entire day listening to other people rant about everything and anything.

You are highly emotional and often moody

An empath feels their emotions and then feels other people's emotions. Naturally, there is going to be a whole lot of moodiness going on. Imagine having to deal with the emotions of six people within an hour. How would that make you feel? Moody, at best and murderous at worst. This is the daily predicament of an empath. They may leave their house feeling all happy and content only to experience six different emotions even before they get to work. If you have a person in your life who seems to have a new emotion every hour, it might be that they are an empath whose feelings are linking with the emotions of other people. Do not judge them unfairly.

You often feel emotionally and mentally drained

As a psychic empath, it is natural to feel depleted at the end of the day when you have used up all the emotional, mental, and physical resources that are available to you. It can be especially daunting if you are working in a situation where you are constantly exposed to people who are in pain or who are upset. What makes it worse is that there are people who consciously drain your energy from you once they figure out that you are an empath. These people are referred to as energy vampires. Chapter 3 delves into the details of how to identify an energy vampire on top of sharing some simple tactics that you can employ to protect yourself when faced with an energy vampire.

Kids and animals naturally gravitate towards you

Kids and pets are not known to be articulate as far as communicating other people's intentions. However, they are both extremely intuitive. What young children and animals lack in communication skills they make up for in intuition. Intuition is defined as the ability to understand instinctively without relying on conscious reasoning. What this means is that a child will instinctively know that you are a good person without going through the steps of logical reasoning. The same case applies to pets. If you are the person that the dog runs to every time even though there are other people in the room, then maybe you need to start looking at yourself more differently. Especially if the other signs of the psychic empath as listed above already apply to you.

You struggle with intimate relationships

As an empath; it is common to struggle with the need to be loved while also wanting to be alone. Togetherness may not be your cup of tea, especially when this togetherness means being overloaded daily. Psychic empaths have to go through a wide range of emotions as they interact with people daily. When they are given a choice to be in a relationship or not, many psychic empaths want the opportunity to be alone just because it's so much easier than being with someone. It's not that they want to be alone forever; it's just that they have gone through the motions of being emotionally drained and they just don't feel like going through it again. It can be quite the delicate balancing act, and many times you will find yourself pushing people away. Some people may assume that you are simply scared of commitment without realizing that you are healing yourself from emotional scars and do not want to take any more on board.

Spirituality resonates with you

There are many different religions in the world with all sorts of rules and ideologies. However, all these strict rules of what you can and cannot do just don't make sense to you. When someone who is gifted with great intuition, they instinctively know what is morally right and wrong and abide their own natural laws that feel right to them. In today's world, the only concept that seems to make sense to the empath is spirituality. Spirituality is a wide concept, giving the empath a sense of freedom, encouraging a path of self-discovery, growth, and connectedness.

Spirituality also expresses the notion that we are apart of

something much bigger than this just this physical world. We are not a human having a physical experience. We are in fact, an eternal soul having a human experience. And this resonates well for the Empath as it ties in with their greater purpose of helping people in the physical world and increasing the Earth consciousness.

You love connecting with nature

Granted, many people love to admire the beauty of the natural world. For you, though, the connection feels deeper and more personal. You love to steal moments at the park, and your ideal home would be a cabin in the woods surrounded by the sights and sounds of the wild. Nature replenishes your energy. You love the greenery of trees, the ocean, and you love to spend your time hiking in the trails. You are never unhappy when you are out and about exploring the natural wonders of the Universe. After getting your energy sapped by those around you, you love the comfort of knowing that nature can restore this energy to the last bit.

You have been accused of being too nice

Empaths really do have hearts of gold. The problem with this is that they do not know when to stop pouring into others. If you are a psychic empath that will give the last shirt on your back, you probably have a few good friends who have picked up on the same. These are the friends who will accuse you of being too nice and tell you that you need to stop giving too much to people because they can see how much it drains you. What your friends may not know is that your generosity is ingrained in your DNA.

You have a very active mind

Most Empaths are quite introverted, which means they are in their head a lot. Thinking, observing, daydreaming, visualizing, reflecting and creating. Empaths view the world entirely different to the average person. This with their gifted intuition, comes a great edge, to create many amazing things to impact the world greatly.

However, this is usually restricted, especially in the empaths early journey from things such as lack of confidence, low self-worth, fear, doubt and uncertainty. Over time as the empath listens to their intuition and focuses on ridding these low vibrational qualities, life becomes exciting.

Struggles of an Empath

As an empath, you will likely have struggles that non-empaths cannot identify with. Simple situations that non-empaths can easily deal with (because they aren't using a whole lot of their emotional resources) will quickly drain you and leave you feeling overwhelmed. Empaths often find themselves struggling on a daily basis, and it can be even harder when you do not already know that you are an empath. As such, you might find yourself questioning why you tend to react in a particular manner when the people around you seem to take everything in their stride.

Mainstream media is overwhelming and draining

While most people look at television as a form of entertainment and a means to unwind after a long day, empaths often have quite the opposite outlook. Television shows can be exceptionally draining for an empath because of the myriad of emotions that producers and directors are aiming to elicit out of their audience. What's more, the news has turned into somewhat of a horror show in itself. Whether news anchors are reporting about the latest Middle East crisis or looming wars between dissenting countries, it only takes minutes before the empath starts their downward spiral into unpleasant emotions.

Empaths don't like saying no

Empaths also often struggle with saying no to others. Most people, empaths or not, do not like to say no to others. There is a certain struggle that comes with denying someone what they want, even when you know it's for the best. It is not for nothing that there are campaigns aimed at helping others know that "no" is a complete statement and answer on its own. When you say no to a person's request, there are often negative feelings that will come by as a result. There might be guilt and even resentment. Empaths hate dealing with negative feelings. They prefer to say "yes" because they like to make other people happy. At the same time, they do not want to deal with any negative emotions that might result from turning down a person's request because then they might be drained by these negative emotions. At the end of the day, empaths find themselves in a rather difficult position where they need to learn to create boundaries by saying no but also protect their energy by learning how to say no in the most tactful way possible.

Empaths struggle with crowds and group interactions

Imagine being able to pick up people's energies just by being in their presence. How would that make you feel? For a moment, it might be fun knowing that you can read someone without even needing to ask what they are feeling. After a while though, you will likely become overwhelmed to the point where you will no longer have any desire to know what a person is going through. This is the life of an empath on a daily basis. When they are out shopping in malls or enjoying a day at the beach, empaths can pick up all the energy around them. This would be fun if all this was positive energy but unfortunately, in most cases, it is not. As such, social situations that provide fun mingling opportunities for non-empaths end up being quite the opposite for them. Often, empaths will choose to retreat to their own solitude. As a result, they get labeled as loners or introverts when in fact they just want to be able to enjoy companionship without getting too overwhelmed.

Empaths are at high risk for addiction

What happens when an empath gets tired of feeling overwhelmed? They look for a way out. An empath who is tired of going through the rollercoaster of emotion and energy will look for something to soothe themselves and quiet the chaos with. In many cases, this ends up being a bad habit, which could eventually turn into an addiction. Many addicts are often empaths who were going through a period of pain and wound up on the wrong path. This is not to mean that all addicts are empaths though. It is important for the psychic empath to replace these bad addictions with 'positive addictions.' For example, learning how to play the guitar or working out at the gym.

Empaths have a hard time holding jobs

Another area that empaths struggle with is the area of employment. Anybody who has ever had a job will easily tell you that jobs are not always fun. There are days when you will show up simply because you need a paycheck. For empaths, this kind of tolerance for something that is not enjoyable might be hard to come by. It is especially daunting for an empath to work in a work environment that is toxic. As such, many empaths struggle to keep jobs and even when they do keep the jobs, they might have a hard time rising to the top. Most people who are non-empaths might find it easy to stay sane in a competitive and brutal workplace where throwing each other under the bus is the norm. However, an empath will struggle with the emotions that come about as a result of this behavior. Empaths will always be on the lookout for jobs that bring them joy and satisfaction. Given the state of the current world, there are not many jobs that suit these criteria and especially not in the corporate realm. As a result, you might find in your life hopping from job to job for reasons that do not make sense to you. Why can't you hold down a job? Blame your heightened sense of empathy. Working for yourself can be a great option for empaths.

Empaths are often tired

Do you often feel tired and fatigued? You just might be facing one of the many struggles of an empath. Many empaths feel exhausted at the end of the day because of the many emotions that they go through when interacting with others. You might find yourself wondering how tired a person who sits at a desk all day might possibly be. Truth is, the office empath will spend eight hours absorbing and dealing with the energy of thier colleagues, only to find themselves absolutely fatigued at the end of the day. When he/she goes home, this empath might find themselves in a space where they continue to absorb the energy of the people they share a home with. If these people are not emitting good energy, the empath will continue to get drained. This will continue even as they sleep (assuming they share a bed with someone), and in the morning they will wake up without the benefit of a refreshing night of sleep. It is easy to see that the empath goes through a never-ending cycle of emotional and mental drain. It can be particularly difficult to maintain a healthy balance of feeling and healing as an empath. If you are always taking on the emotions of others without prioritizing yourself, there is a high chance that you will burn yourself out.

Many people like to take advantage of empaths

Even when they do not mean to put themselves in that

predicament, empaths often find themselves as the delegated dumping ground for all kinds of emotional garbage. Friends, family, colleagues and even strangers often use empaths as their platforms for unloading every emotional and mental baggage that they may have. Since empaths rarely say no (and are such good listeners), they are often left to mop up the mess left behind, while the other party moves on with the relief of having gotten something off their chest.

They struggle to articulate who or what they are

A lot of psychic empaths struggle with their self-identity. This is often a result of the conflicting, and often demeaning, messages that they have heard about themselves all their lives. When a psychic empath grows up in a household that they are not listened to or dismissed as being dramatic or too emotional, they retreat into a shell for protection purposes. In this shell, the psychic empath wonders about who they are.

Am I really just too emotional?

Am I being too dramatic? Am I overreacting?

Am I right in behaving in this manner or will I come off as being too sensitive?

What is wrong with being too sensitive anyway?

These are all questions that an empath might struggle with. Such questions breed self-doubt and self-doubt is often the root cause of low self-worth and identity issues, which are all struggles that empaths commonly face.

They may struggle with depression and anxiety

Because of the myriad emotions that psychic empath goes through, and the fact that they rarely get any support for it, there is a high chance for the development of depression and anxiety. Of course, this is not to say that psychic empaths are all depressed and anxious. The truth of the matter; however, is that psychic empaths are highly predisposed to depression and anxiety because they are essentially emotional sponges. They mop up emotional spills and keep them in. When these spills accumulate inside the empath with no healthy outlet, there is a significant risk for depression and other mood disorders.

They struggle with personal relationships

Imagine being able to pick up the feelings of everyone around you. How would this change your perception of relationships? You might be unwilling to get too close to people because you find them too much to handle. You might be unable to confront the feelings that you arouse in other people, especially when these feelings are those of discomfort, sadness, anger or even hate. In short, you might not do very well with getting close to people. Couple this with the fact that many empaths are introverted and live inside their heads and you have yourself a recipe that does not allow for very many personal or intimate relationships. While the empath may want to feel close and loved, they like their downtime a lot too. Striking a balance between being loved and being left alone is definitely something that many empaths struggle with.

Dealing with Narcissists

It is not uncommon for an empath to have experienced or dealt with a narcissist in their life. In most cases, it is either experienced by a narcissistic parent or narcissistic partner or both. As we know, empaths have supreme empathy. Narcissists, however, are incapable of expressing any signs of empathy. To the narcissist, people are viewed as objects that can be manipulated as if they were on a chess board in order to serve the narcissists very own needs. Empaths seem to find themselves entangled frequently in the narcissist's web of deception purely because it is so easy for the narcissist to manipulate them, especially if the empath is early in the process of self-discovery.

Overcoming narcissists, however, is a natural part of the process as we are able to recognize red flags much better in the future and ensure greater protection. They also reflect our weak points that we need to work on in order to become a more empowered individual. An empowered empath will not be susceptible to the manipulation and mind tactics of a narcissist.

Chapter 2: Types of Psychic Empaths

Psychic empaths are not all alike. There are different types of psychic empaths, depending on how they sense energy around them. The six different types of psychic empaths include the emotional empath, the claircognizant empath, the geomantic empath, the telepathic empath, the precognitive empath, and the psychometric empath.

Emotional Empath

This is the most common type of psychic empath. An emotional empath is able to pick up the emotions of the people around them very easily. They can feel the sadness of a sad person and the joy of a happy person as if those two emotions were their own. If an emotional empath is not self-aware and able to differentiate their feelings and those of others, then they can become emotionally drained very quickly. If you consider yourself an emotional empath, it is important that you learn to step back and take care of yourself so that you do not get mentally or emotionally drained.

Claircognizant Empath

Sometimes referred to as an intuitive empath, the claircognizant empath is able to read other people just by being in their presence. Claircognizant empaths are hard to lie to because they can recognize lies even though the person is trying their best to mask their intentions. If you are able to look at a person and immediately sense the energies of deceit around them then you just might be a claircognizant empath. If you are this type of empath, you will prefer to surround yourself with people who have good and clean energy that aligns with your own.

Besides being able to easily read people's intentions, you will know that you have claircognizance if you seem to experience coincidences more than the average person. For example, you might pick up your phone to call your best friend only for the phone to start ringing. The name on the caller ID? Your best friend. You also seem to be brimming with new and wonderful ideas that you cannot wait to share with others. Claircognizant empaths are often very artistic and creative. They make for very good musicians and writers because they can sense what other people want, and then articulate this perfectly.

Geomantic Empath

A geomantic empath has the ability to read and recognize the energies given off by the planet. In other words, they can communicate with the environment around them. How do you know if you are a geomantic empath? A key sign to look out for is when you feel a strong connection towards a place or if a particular place strongly repels you. It could be because you are picking up energy that you either like a lot or strongly resent from a particular place. Geomantic empaths tend to have the ability to tell when a natural disaster is oncoming. For instance, they might sense when a tsunami is on the way even before the meteorological department issues an alarm. Many animals tend to have geomantic empathy. They will, for instance, run and hide for cover before the onset of a tsunami.

Telepathic Empath

In the simplest terms, a telepathic empath is a mind reader. They can tell what is going on in another person's mind without needing to be told. A telepathic empath may also be able to read the needs of entities that are not in a position to communicate the same. For instance, plants and animals. This paranormal ability of the telepathic empath makes it possible for them to tell when someone is telling lies. They can easily read the lies as they tumble up and down the person's mind. It is important to note that a person may be a telepath and not necessarily an empath. Where these two concepts of telepathy and empathy intersect you have a telepathic empath. On its own telepathy is the ability to read minds. It is a concept that has been greatly argued, with an equal number of proponents and opponents.

Psychometric Empath

Psychometric empaths are able to pick up energy from inanimate objects such as clothing. They can tell the emotions and experiences that a person went through simply by touching an item of clothing previously worn by that person. If you have watched television shows about missing persons where psychics are contacted by the victim's family to try and find out what happened to that person, then you most likely have watched a psychometric empath at work.

How can you tell if you are a psychometric empath? You will know if you are a psychometric empath if you find yourself drawn or repelled by objects based on the energy they emit. While other people are able to go through life not bothered by things like chairs, scarves, cups and other inanimate objects, you will find yourself hating the presence of these things if they give off negative energy. Of course, this might not be the kind of thing that you will easily open up to people about. It might seem strange to a colleague to tell them that you dislike the energy that the coffee maker gives or that you are getting strange vibes from the photocopier. However, knowing that you are not going crazy and that psychometric empathy is indeed real should bring you some sense of comfort.

Precognitive Empath

A precognitive empath has the ability to experience an event before it happens. Often, this experience will be in the form of a premonition or a strong foreboding. Precognitive empaths experienced a sudden shift in mood or physical experience when they are undergoing these experiences. This could happen during waking hours or in a dream. If you have ever had a bad feeling that preceded a disaster or tragic event, then you experienced something that is referred to as precognition, which in other words is what a precognitive empath goes through on an almost daily basis. This gift can be used to predict and avert disaster, especially when the empath takes time to practice using their gift. This gift can also present itself positively. For example, you may get an insight into a place you will be traveling to in the future, or the arrival of a newborn baby in the family.

Chapter 3: Key Enemies of an Empath

If you ever encounter an energy vampire in your life, you will feel it even before you know it. How so? Energy vampires have a way of taking away all the good energy from other people's lives and replacing it with feelings of emotional drain. Some energy vampires do this deliberately, while others are unknowing about the destruction caused by their negative energy and presence. Regardless of whether an energy vampire is intentional or not, you must learn how to identify one and how to handle being around one.

Let's start by defining what an energy vampire is. An energy vampire is a person that feeds off other people's energy. Often, an energy vampire is an emotionally immature individual who is unable to feel their own energy voids and therefore looks to others for fulfillment. When a person that is emotionally mature and stable experiences certain feelings such as anger or sadness, they often try to process these feelings by themselves. Energy vampires do not have this capacity. Instead of sifting through their emotions, they project these onto others. In the process, they steal away all the good energy from others and replace it with their own emotions of anger, sadness, despair, and other negative feelings.

Dealing with an energy vampire can be extremely draining, especially when you are not aware of the fact that they are an energy vampire. There will be many times when you will wonder why you always feel a particular kind of way after spending time in the company of a certain individual. You might wonder whether you are being unfair and judging that person harshly. What you might not know is that you are right to feel that way because the person in question is an energy vampire who always manages to take you to the brink of emotional exhaustion.

Energy vampires come in different forms. Knowing how to tell them apart is the first step towards ensuring they are no longer capable of stealing your emotional resources from you. The main types of energy vampires, otherwise known as emotional vampires, are: the melodramatic vampire, the victim, the narcissist, the intimidator, judgmental, and the innocent vampires.

The Melodramatic Vampire

The melodramatic vampire feeds off drama. They cannot exist in a place where there is no drama. This kind of energy vampire thrives on blowing everything out of proportion and must always be the main character in every show. If you are in a relationship with this kind of person, you will always find yourself caught up in one public scene or another. Outbursts will be a common occurrence and you will often catch yourself in cringeworthy public encounters. Melodramatic vampires do not care who gets swept up in their wave of conflict and heightened emotion. They only care that they get the attention they want when they want it. At work, a melodramatic vampire might take the form of a colleague who is always making a big deal out of every little thing that they do. You will catch this colleague in the office kitchen and at the printer's complaining about how hard their life is because of one thing or another. You might even hear them whine on and on about how late they were in getting home because another colleague did something that inconvenienced them, however minor that might have been.

Why do melodramatic vampires behave this way? Most people who seek attention at whatever cost do so because it validates them. These are often the kind of people who, for one reason or the other, never learned how to be comfortable with their own selves without the need for external validation. This could be as a result of being neglected as a child or because they grew up believing the world revolves around them. Either way, the child may grow up thinking that they are owed attention and that the only way to feel whole is by making sure that the entire world is watching them.

If you are faced with a drama queen or a melodramatic energy vampire, the very first thing you need to know is this: you do not owe anybody your time or attention. They are very few people on this Earth that you are obliged to give your attention and time. Your children, for instance, rank highly on the list of people who can reasonably demand to be made a priority in your life. You are also worthy of the attention and time that you so effortlessly give to others. Outside of those two, you get to choose who gets your time and who gets cut off.

A good thing about people who love drama is that they are easy to spot. Soon after meeting a person, you will be able to tell whether they thrive on drama. You can spot it in the way they approach conflict and the way they carry themselves in public. If a person is always screaming and yelling and demanding to see the manager at every turn, run away and don't look back. This is the same sort of person that will burn the house and throw cooking pans at you because an old acquaintance texted you at ten o'clock at night, without first determining the reason for the text message.

If you are unable to walk away from someone that loves drama, for example, if it is a colleague or boss that you must work with, the important thing to remember is not to encourage their drama. Do not get tempted to participate in their shouting matches. Do not say things that feed their drama. As long as a melodramatic vampire is not getting anything in return, they will not be able to keep up their show for too long. The energy they seek will not be available for them to steal. In the case of a family member who is a drama vampire, limit the amount of time that you spend with them. Just because someone is related to you does not mean that they are allowed to get away with bad behavior.

The Victim Vampire

The victim is always easy to identify. They like to play the supporting role in every bad circumstance in their life. They do not take responsibility for anything and always have a finger ready to point at someone else. An energy vampire that takes on the role of a victim can be identified by their love for complaints and their complete lack of responsibility. In their world, nothing is ever their fault. Everyone else is to be blamed for their actions and they will complain about anything and everything under the sun. Oh, and don't even bother wasting your time trying to get an apology out of them. They feed off the pity that they elicit from others every time they share their woes. While it is important to be sympathetic to the suffering of others, you must be careful about the kind of attention that you show towards the victim. If you show too much sympathy, the victim will never leave you alone. They will always keep coming back in the hope that you will show them some of this sympathy that they have gotten used to. Unlike the drama vampire that you might easily cut off without a second thought, the victim might be harder to get rid of. This is simply because you might feel guilty about abandoning someone who is in need of your help but you must know that these people love to take advantage.

If the victim in your life is someone that you really care about, consider helping them set some goals in their life that can make them feel as if they are in control. Ensure that you put in place measures of accountability that will help determine whether they are being responsible and working towards their goals. For instance, if you have a sister that is always complaining about their finances, consider helping them to set up a savings or investment account. Have them contribute a portion of their paycheck to this account every month. By doing this, you will have changed the narrative from one of pity to one where the victim feels empowered to do something about their life.

Otherwise, if you have an energy vampire in your life that loves to whine about everything, does not take responsibility for their own actions and that you are not particularly invested in, feel free to cut them out of your life. Limit the amount of time you spend around them and you will begin to feel your energy levels peaking again.

The Narcissist Vampire

Narcissism is a personality disorder that is characterized by an inflated sense of self-importance, entitlement, and an obsession with one's physical appearance. Narcissists believe that they are the best thing since sliced bread and will often go to great lengths to prove this point. They do not take kindly to criticism, and they often do not care about what other people have to say unless it is said in admiration. Perhaps you've already encountered one of these types of energy vampires into your life since they love empaths.

Finding yourself in a relationship, be it romantic or work, with a narcissist can be one of the most daunting things you will ever go through. You will spend your life placating the ego of the narcissist and saying yes to all their demands, while your needs fall on deaf ears. A narcissist will steal all the joy and air from a room and then blame you for it. They will want to control every aspect of your life and make it their own domain.

Out of all energy vampires, the narcissist might be the most dangerous based on the lengths that they are willing to go to maintain the status quo. Because they are incapable of feeling empathy, the narcissist will not even care that you are facing emotional drain because of them. They simply cannot relate to your predicament however much you try to show them that you are getting beaten down by their negative energy.

When you find yourself faced with a person who exhibits the qualities of a narcissist vampire, the first thing you should do is consider the possibility of cutting them out of your life. This might be easy in some instances and harder in others. For instance, if you are just getting started on a romantic relationship and notice the signs of narcissism, it will be easier to leave because you are not invested. What happens when the signs start showing up four years into a marriage? It might be harder to just walk away. It is even harder when it is your boss who is the narcissistic vampire.

When dealing with a narcissistic boss, for instance, you will need to be very smart about your approach. One of the things you can do is make sure that you never allow them to get under your skin. Do not give the narcissist the satisfaction of knowing that they will always get a reaction out of you. This is what drives a narcissist—knowing that they can push you to the point where you explode. If you never explode, you will have denied them the ending that they so yearn for. Another way to protect yourself is to avoid argument so that you never give them a chance to twist your words against you. Narcissists will take advantage of every word that comes out of your mouth to ensure that they have the upper hand. As long as you do not say anything, you will have denied them the ammunition that they are so desperate to have.

Do not feel the pressure to massage your boss' ego just because they are a narcissist that thrives on it. It is tempting to play along with the narcissist just for the sake of keeping the peace. Many employees quickly learn that they can get favors from their boss by saying the things that their boss wants to hear. Always remember that you were hired because of the skills and value that you bring to the table, and you do not need to dance to the tune of your boss just because it makes him or her feel better when you do. It is not your job to appease the insecurities of your narcissistic boss because insecurities are in fact the root cause of the narcissist's behavior.

What happens then if the narcissist vampire in your life is someone that you love, or are romantically involved in, or maybe even a family member? Loving a narcissist can be very draining, especially because you often get nothing in return. Narcissists do not know how to love others. They love themselves and they love the things that other people do for them. They are also experts at wearing down the people who love them, mentally and emotionally so that they are never able to detect their manipulative ways.

If you are caught up in a relationship with a narcissist who is willing to change (and this is very rare), consider going into professional counseling and establishing boundaries that help you maintain a healthy union.

If the narcissistic vampire in your life is unwilling to change and is constantly abusive, walk away and do not look back. In many cases, abusive narcissists only get worse, so do not stick around hoping that things will get better. You will only be setting yourself up for failure if you refuse to prioritize your well-being, which is exactly what the narcissistic vampire is counting on.

For a more in depth guide on understanding narcissists and how to escape being in a relationship with a narcissist, you can check out my other book: *Narcissism and Narcissistic Abuse Recovery: Free Yourself by Understanding the Narcissists Personality Disorder, What the Hell Happened in Your Relationship, and How to Effectively Heal.*

The Intimidator Vampire

Have you ever met someone who behaved as if they had a point to prove? If you have answered yes to this question, then high chances are that you have encountered an intimidator vampire. Intimidator vampires have deep-seated insecurities that they constantly battle with. They feel weak, small, and intimidated by life and everything around them. They reiterate and compensate by trying to make the people around them feel these things in return. As such, they are hell-bent on making others look weak and inferior and unworthy. The intimidator vampire will often hold bigoted views on things, especially when this bigotry is shared within a group that makes him think he is better than he actually is. Such vampires are also racist and will commit hate crimes against others, especially while in groups. The biggest identifier of an intimidator vampire is the fact that they are unable to hold their own when confronted. They thrive by hiding behind ridiculous beliefs and in numbers. They can never stand up in front of a group of people and say the things they do unless they have the backing of their fellow bigots. You will be able to spot an intimidator vampire based on their loudmouth and often obnoxious behavior.

When dealing with an intimidator vampire, the first thing you need to realize is that their attempt to make you feel inferior stems from their deep feelings of inferiority. They are not actually as aggressive and confident as they want to come across. In the confines and safety of their homes, intimidator vampires are like scared little cats that want a hug. However, it is not your job to give this level of comfort. Intimidator vampires could benefit from professional counseling so that they can confront their feelings of unworthiness. Another practical step to take when dealing with this vampire is to agree to disagree. Accept the fact that you can hold divergent views without getting in each other's faces about it. Do not try to argue with an intimidator vampire. They will beat you at it by being loud and saying the most outrageous things. Lastly, do not engage unless you absolutely have to. Whenever possible, walk away before things escalate. The intimidator vampire can especially say very hurtful things because they are looking to hurt those around them. If you do not want to get caught up in this, simply walk away and refuse to engage.

Judgmental Vampire

Why are some people so judgmental? You probably know a few judgmental people in your life. They always have something to say about everything, even when nobody has asked for their opinion. They will pick apart other people's relationships, their choice of attire, their lifestyle choices, their career decisions and all of these will fall short. It is often impossible to please a judgmental person. Nothing you do will ever measure up to their standards. Having a judgmental spouse or parent can be particularly discouraging, especially when you are trying your best to be the best version of yourself.

So, again, why are some people so judgmental? To put it succinctly, judgment often comes about as a result of what is within a person, and less as a result of what is going on around them. It has been said that we hate most in others those things that remind us of ourselves. This is the driving force behind judgment. You may not even be conscious about it but the trauma that you experience will always be at the back of your mind guiding your emotions and turning you into the judgmental person that you said you'd never be.

Some people are often unable to separate the action from the doer, and as such will always have a finger to point even without understanding the context of the act. When this is coupled with a lack of empathy, it can be particularly difficult to be anything but judgmental.

If you have a judgmental vampire in your life, be careful not to take everything that they say personally. Understand that the jabs thrown your way may just be symptoms of some underlying hurt that the vampire is dealing with. This does not mean that you need to take everything lying down. Consider calling out the vampire on their behavior, but ever so sweetly so that it does not become a shouting match. Being firm and solid in your truth about who you are will also help to ensure that you are not overly affected by the criticism of other people. If all else fails, cut out the judgmental vampire from your life. Life is too short to stick around people who are always trying to put you down. Surround yourself with positive energy.

The Innocent or Unknowing Vampire

Some people drain us without meaning to. They simply come to us with their needs and problems because it is the only thing they know. Your children, for instance, will constantly turn to you for support and reassurance without being aware of the fact that they drain you or that you need someone to support and reassure you as well. Good friends may also be the unknowing vampires in your life if they are constantly looking to you to provide the emotional support that can only come from a friend.

With the innocent vampire, it is important to remember that one of the most effective ways of helping someone is by showing them how to solve their own problems. If your child is always coming to you with the same problem, show them how to solve it. Empower them so that they are less reliant on you. At the same time, learn to take some time out for yourself. Mothers, in particular, have this overwhelming sense of guilt every time they check out of parenting for a few hours to have some time for themselves. Motherhood is a tough job and to do well at it you will need to set aside moments where you focus solely on your self-care, unapologetically and with no guilt. When it comes to your friends, you will need to set boundaries and let them find their own wings as well. While it is great to be known as the friend that always shows up for others, you also need to show up for yourself. This is the only way you will remain in good form without feeling the effects of being drained by the unknowing vampires in your life.

Signs of Emotional Exhaustion

The thing about emotional exhaustion, otherwise known as emotional drain, is that it can often be disguised as something else. For example, you might experience emotional drain in the form of headaches. When this happens, you may be tempted to chalk it up to dehydration, exhaustion or just the everyday stress of your work. The fact is that emotional drain often creeps up on you, only for you to realize one day that you are completely and totally exhausted. You will try to look back and think back to when the emotional drain started, and you will likely be unable to pinpoint the exact moment. As an empath, you may sense another person's negative energy and the impact it has on you, and yet be unable to consciously recognize the cumulative effects of that energy. Just as you are sensitive to other people's needs and emotional states, you will also need to be aware of your own needs and the state of your emotional health. Look out for the signs of emotional drain and take appropriate measures before it spirals out of control.

Insomnia/ Difficulty Falling Asleep

Insomnia is perhaps one of the loudest signals of emotional exhaustion. When your mind is filled with stress and worries, it becomes almost impossible to fall asleep. The mind requires a certain state of calmness and relaxation so that it can settle into a state that is conducive for sleep. An emotionally exhausted person is at a place where all the emotion centers in their brain are fired up. They are like little flickering lights that refuse to go out, even when it's time for bed. Pay attention to insomnia when it comes calling. It is often a clear sign that something is wrong in your life. Nobody stays up at night tossing and turning when they are emotionally healthy and happy in their life.

If you are having trouble sleeping, there are certain steps that you can take to make this a thing of the past. Of course, eliminating the stressors in your life (also known as energy vampires) should be your go-to step every time you catch yourself falling down the black hole that is emotional drain. However, we have so far determined that getting rid of energy vampires is not always possible depending on the type of relationship that we have with them. So, in the case of insomnia, there are several tips that you can apply to remedy the situation.

First, learn to switch off from your job when you leave the office. Do not carry the stresses of one place to the next place. By doing so, you will be allowing yourself to carry all the negative aura of the workplace environment and transfer it to your home, which should be your safe and happy place. Whenever possible, do not carry your work home. Many employees will lay awake at night worried about the pending report in their laptop without knowing that their emotional health supersedes the importance of that report. Seriously, leave work at work and enjoy your time at home. You are not what is holding the company together. Your report is not what will cause the company to come crashing down. Learn to take life in your own stride. If someone calls you after work hours for something related to work, make sure the phone call is brief and forget about the matter as soon as the conversation ends.

A relaxing bath infused with essential oils also does the trick when it comes to combating insomnia. Water is a friend to an empath. Water cleanses all the dirt and bad energy of an empath and leaves them feeling invigorated and ready for a peaceful night of restful sleep. Couple this with some chamomile tea and sleep meditation and you will be off to slumberland before you know it.

Lack of Motivation

When you started at your job, you were full of energy and ready to take on any assignments coming your way. Three months down the line, you are struggling to wake up for the very job you used to love. What changed? Well, you had several run-ins with your manager who happens to be a quintessential narcissist. This manager has managed to wear you down every step of the way. They criticize your work, put you down in front of others, and do not seem to have a single kind word to say about you. You have started struggling with your self-esteem and can feel your voice becoming quieter and quieter, where before it used to be bold and confident. A lack of motivation is a clear sign of emotional exhaustion. When you are constantly beat down emotionally it becomes almost impossible to be excited about things anymore.

You will know that your motivation has taken a hit when the things that used to excite you start to feel like chores. Because your emotional energy has been depleted, you have nothing left to give to the things that matter. Take a look around you. How is your living situation? Do you live in a clean house? Do you make your bed when you wake up? Can you honestly say that you treat yourself well by taking care of your hygiene, your health, your diet and anything else that relates to you? Were there days that you have treated yourself better? If yes, what changed? What are your goals in life? Do you see yourself putting in the conscious effort every day towards the achievement of these goals?

Taking stock of your current circumstances, and how much you have contributed to these, is a great first step towards determining whether you are motivated or not. Intrinsic motivation is a hallmark of an emotionally intelligent person. Emotional intelligence is a concept that an empath must learn if they are looking to manage those around them. The good news is that, as an empath, you already have the empathy part of emotional intelligence figured out. You only need to work on the other components, which include motivating yourself internally so that you really show up externally.

Anger and Irritability

When do you find yourself most irritable and likely to snap at the smallest things? More often than not, you will be prone to anger when you are going through a stressful event. When you are emotionally drained, you will not have the capacity for the patience that would be expected from a normal and logical person. Small things that you could previously have ignored will set you off and you will not be able to keep your cool in situations. Most people are smart enough to know that anger comes from a place of fear, hurt, and even frustration. These are all feelings that come about with emotional exhaustion. You'll never see a happy person lashing out at another. If you have been short-fused recently, consider evaluating whether you have also been going through a moment of emotional turmoil. You are probably not an angry person but simply a good person who got pushed too far and for too long.

Detachment

What happens to an empath who has been subjected to torrents of emotional abuse by the energy vampires in their life? They learn to steer clear, and with this steering clear comes a sense of detachment. Being pushed to the point of emotional drain is a type of trauma, and trauma often breeds coping strategies. Emotional detachment is a form of coping strategy. A person that is emotionally detached will struggle to form connections because they have unknowingly switched off their emotions to protect themselves.

Detachment could be towards people or even towards your own passions. You might find yourself feeling no desire or interest in a specific topic that previously excited you, simply because you are shielding yourself from the heartbreak and emotional fatigue of failure. You may also subconsciously choose to distance yourself from people because you have faced emotional exhaustion every time you get close to someone.

Pay attention any time you start to feel as if you are going numb where emotions are concerned. This is your wake-up call that something is not right. Nobody was meant to go through life not feeling any sense of joy or happiness from anything. If you catch yourself feeling numb and unexcitable about things, talk to someone. You might be totally drained and tired of putting up a fight. Professional help or even a kind listening ear just might give you the jumpstart you need to start feeling again. And remember, if the emotional drain that caused you to start feeling completely detached and numb comes from something that you do not have to have in your life, kick the stressor out. This includes your job. There is no paycheck on this Earth that is worth your emotional health.

Physical Pains

Emotional drain sometimes shows up in the form of physical pain. There are some tell-tale physical signs that suggest that someone is in the throes of burnout. These include constant inexplicable headaches or migraines and even dizziness. You might even start to experience shortness of breath and heart palpitations. All these physical symptoms point to an underlying problem of emotional fatigue and possible anxiety, which is both a symptom and a result of emotional drain. When faced with physical pain, your first stop should be your doctor's office. This will help you ascertain that there is nothing physically wrong with you. If that is the case, then you can move on to the next step of identifying all the energy vampires that have driven you to the point of emotional drain. Most doctors will not shy away from giving their honest assessment of the situation, especially when they realize that there is no physical cause for your symptoms. Many physicians are well aware of the tribulations that a lot of people go through in their everyday lives and are able to identify the symptoms of emotional drain from a mile off.

Lots of Crying

Granted, empaths are likely to cry a lot. There is always something waiting around the corner to tug at their heartstrings. It could be a cute video of a kitten or a baby taking their first steps and the empath will suddenly find themselves overcome with emotion. Being highly emotional is the empath's giveaway. However, if you suddenly find yourself bursting into tears in the middle of the day about nothing in particular, you might be going through emotional drain.

Crying is a good thing. A good well-timed cry can be extremely therapeutic. A happy cry, on the other hand, is always welcome and hardly makes anybody uncomfortable. However, if you are spontaneously crying in the middle of the day, in the subway, at work, during lunch or when you are printing your reports, then you might need to sit down and take stock of your emotional health. There is some science behind crying: when a human being is experiencing strong and overwhelming emotions, be that of sadness or joy, the limbic system picks up these emotions and sends a signal to the autonomic nervous system. In return, the nervous system activates the tear glands, or turns on the waterworks if you like, resulting in a good cry. An emotionally drained person is in a state of great emotional duress. They will go through their day experiencing extremely strong emotions because they are completely worn out. Your limbic system does not know that you are in the middle of a meeting, so it will simply pick up on these emotions and then send the necessary signals to the nervous system.

Hopelessness

A great singer once asked, where do broken hearts go? A good rejoinder to that question would be, where do hopeless minds go? Hope is the fire that keeps you moving even when you are not certain of how tomorrow will be. Can you feel that fire in your belly right now? If not, what happened to that fire? What took it away?

In the face of emotional exhaustion, it can be impossible to feel hopeful about anything. The mind is a powerful organ. In fact, the mind is the most powerful organ and tool that a human being possesses. In your mind, you can conceive ideas and decide what you want to be. You can overcome tribulations simply by telling your mind that you will. Many people have become great and left lasting legacies simply because they put their mind to it. There is nothing that you cannot do when your mind is in a good place. Hopelessness stems from a mind that is in a bad place. When your mind and emotion have been corrupted by the negative energies of energy vampires, you find yourself stuck with a vast plain of darkness and hopelessness. Everywhere you look seems bleak. Your dreams do not matter. Your suffering seems endless. You do not have hope that tomorrow will be better than today. You cannot see a way out. Narcissists are especially great at pushing their victims towards hopelessness because they know that this is a very effective way of shackling someone to their status quo. A narcissist vampire will constantly tell you that there is no life beyond your current circumstances. They will tell you that there is no better job than the one you have (if they are your boss) and that there is no one who could ever love you if you leave them (if they are your partner). The important thing is to recognize these statements as the blatant lies that they are. These lies are designed to get you feeling hopeless so that you can be easily worn down and made to do exactly as an energy vampire wants you to do.

Chapter 4: Thriving as a Psychic Empath

If you are an empath who wants to take back control in your life, you will be pleased to know that there are some short-term strategies that you can use. These are things that you can do in your everyday life, starting now, to feel better and be more in control of your energy.

Learn to Say No and Walk Away

One of the simplest tips to managing your energy field as an empath is learning to say "No" and walking away when negative energy enters your space. In your everyday life and interactions, there will be instances where you begin to feel your energy draining away. For instance, you might be in an environment where two argumentative colleagues are beginning to clutter your space with negative energy. At this point, it is best to walk away and remove yourself from that environment. It is important to do so without being apologetic. As an empath, you are often worried about offending other people. The problem with this type of mindset is that it puts you in unpleasant situations instead. When walking away from a toxic situation, do so without feeling the need to apologize and without worrying about who gets offended. Unapologetically protecting your energy is vital.

Just Breathe

At this point in the book, we have already determined that empaths tend to hate crowds. So, what happens when you find yourself in a situation where being part of a crowd is inevitable? If you cannot avoid a situation that calls for a gathering of a large group of people, then make sure you position yourself in a way where you are at the lowest risk of emotional drain. Standing in the center of a crowd only makes you highly vulnerable to energy drain from the energy vampires surrounding you from all sides. A safer position would be at the edge of the crowd, somewhere in a corner where some bits of you are partially hidden from the energy signals coming from the crowd.

Breathing deeply is yet another way an empath can deal with their emotions when they start to feel overwhelmed. A deep breath can center and ground you when you start to feel drained and bombarded by the different energy signals that you receive from those around you. A deep exhale from the mouth serves to expel the bad energy from within you, while an inhale through the nose replaces this with the clean energy from nature. Breathing in and out is also a meditation trick that is aimed at helping you become more conscious of your emotions. A deep breath can calm your nerves and get rid of anger in an instant. Next time someone is projecting their anger onto you, take a quick breath and allow yourself to feel the good energy taking center stage in your body.

Limit Physical Contact

As a psychic empath, you are able to receive the energy of the people around you through eye contact and even physical contact. This means that the more you touch and interact with people, the more likely you are to receive the energy that they have within them. As much as possible, limit the amount of physical contact that you allow in your life, at least until you are sure that you will not be receiving bad energy from a particular person. It is within your rights as a human being to refuse to give hugs to strangers or even particular friends and colleagues, especially if these individuals make you feel drained after every hug. Sometimes, even the most well-meaning people can drain your energy through physical contact if they are needy and constantly seeking physical affection and affirmation. Stay-at-home moms who spend all day with small kids who are constantly clawing at them to be picked up and tended to know how draining it can be to always be on the giving end for physical affection. At the end of the day, such moms only want to be left alone without any physical touch. Empaths tend to have the same problem when it comes to constant physical touch. In the same breath, reenergizing physical touch can be very powerful to the empath. An empath must; therefore, figure out the people who are great for hugging and those that must be avoided.

Make Time for Alone Time

Creating alone time is another crucial strategy that an empath must have if they are to survive living in a crowded world where escaping other people's energies is almost impossible. Alone time is one of the best ways to fully recharge and get ready to face another day for the empath. During this alone time, you may choose to do whatever makes you happy. You can read a book or watch a wholesome movie. You can even take a nap or soak in a bubble bath. The only person who can make the rules of alone time is you, depending on what you like best. However, the key thing to take into consideration is that alone time with your smartphone does not count as alone time. The smartphone is one of the top enemies of an empath. Not only do smartphones interfere with the ability to sleep thanks to their blue light, they are also awash with depressing information and social media trolls who rank highly as energy vampires. Always remember to put your phone onto airplane mode before going into alone time. Calls and text messages should not be answered, while you are enjoying your solitude. Any emails that come through during your moment of peace must remain unanswered. Learning to switch off and just bask in the quiet is one of the greatest gifts you will ever give yourself as an empath.

Say Goodbye to TV and Facebook

Another great tactic that will help in your survival as an empath is switching off the television and staying off the Internet. The television and the Internet are both great channels for accessing information. Unfortunately, they are often filled with a lot of negative energy that can be debilitating for the empath that soaks everything in. While it might be beneficial to watch television and access the Internet every once in a while, it is very easy to over-consume irrelevant information and going overboard is only going to wear you down. A good way to go about this is to set aside time for accessing the internet and TV. This allows you to monitor the kind of information that is being sent your way and put an end to things when you start to feel drained. Staying off social media is also a good idea. Facebook, Instagram, Snapchat and other social media platforms help us stay connected to our friends and family but are also highly detrimental when abused. If you are able to call the people you love on the phone and talk to them, then there really is no need to have numerous social media pages that expose you to the negativity of the online community.

Prioritize Yourself

As an empath, it is normal and natural to always put the needs of others ahead of yours. You are born to be a giver. It is part of who you are. In fact, giving is the essence of who you are. To survive in a world that is almost always taking without giving anything in return you will need to learn how to be selfish. It is ok to put yourself first. In fact, according to airline safety instructions you are supposed to put on the oxygen mask first before attempting to help others. In everyday life, this means that you should always take care of yourself first before taking care of others. This makes perfect sense as you cannot pour from an empty cup. Train yourself to prioritize yourself first. It is ok to worry about yourself first and to care about yourself first before caring about the next person. You might feel guilty for a while, but you will soon realize that you are in a better position to give to others when you give to yourself first.

Visualization for Protection

Visualization is the art of taking your mind on an adventure. Instead of just thinking about your current environment, visualization allows you to remove yourself from that state and think of something much better. A good way to utilize visualization in protecting your energy is to imagine yourself encased by an impenetrable shield that protects you from all the negative energy of the world. You could even visualize a fierce lioness guarding your personal space and running off all energy vampires. This technique comes in handy when you suddenly realize you are in the presence of an energy vampire, especially the innocent vampire. With the innocent vampire, you may be halfway into a conversation before you realize how invested you are and how drained you feel. This is a perfect time to use visualization to protect and regain your energy and stop fully investing in the conversation.

Be Grateful for Your Gift

Empathy is a great thing. It is not a burden that you have been cursed with. Being an empath is a great gift that has been bestowed on you so that you can heal yourself and others. When you are in the trenches dealing with heavy emotions, empathy can feel like the worst thing to have. You might have days when you wish you weren't capable of feeling as you do. There will be moments when you will be envious of your less empathetic friends, and their ability to shrug off things and events as if they did not happen. Even in these moments, remember that you are greatly blessed and highly gifted. Gratitude is a good way to train your mind to see your empathy as a good thing rather than a heavy burden. Psychologists have studied the human mind and found that being grateful has a way of lifting depressed spirits. In fact, people who are often dealing with depression are told to write down three things that they are grateful for every day. After several weeks of consistently expressing gratitude, most people report happier and lighter spirits. If your spirit is heavy about the fact that you are an empath, consider keeping a notebook where you can write down three things that you are grateful for every day. It could be the fact that your intuition saved you from doing something or how you were able to lift someone else's spirits at work. Either way, you will soon start to realize that what you have is a good thing that should be cherished, regardless of how it feels on some days.

Consume Positive Material

Being an empath can be challenging at times and the quickest path to becoming a psychic empath warrior is to indulge in the world of self-development. Whilst there is an overwhelming amount of useless information out there, there is also a plethora of incredible knowledge out there in the form of books and audiobooks. A book can be a worthwhile companion when you are struggling with an unruly mind because it engages your attention on a new set of ideas or skills for you to learn. And even if you do not like reading, you can still indulge in a good audiobook on your commute to or from work. Audiobooks are especially great in ensuring that you do not get lost in your own thoughts, as you have someone right there reading to you, ensuring you do not tune out and go to that quiet place that empaths love to retreat to. As you continue to learn new information over time, you will be surprised at how much of an impact this will have on your life.

Chapter 5: Long-Term Survival Strategies

As an empath, you will need long-term survival strategies that will help you cope with living in a world that is highly demanding and full of negative energy without getting overwhelmed. Unlike the shorter-term strategies that were discussed in Chapter 4, the long-term strategies will require a little bit of practice and persistence. Incorporating these strategies in your everyday life will help you become a better person who can take care of themselves and impact the world around you without losing yourself. And don't worry, some people might say that you are changing, that you are becoming more selfish and inaccessible or that they do not know who you are anymore. Do not take these statements too seriously. Part of growth is discarding the old bits about us that no longer work for us and bringing onboard new tactics that help us become the best versions of ourselves.

Define Your Needs as a Person

One of the very first things you will need to do is define what your needs and desires are as a human being. Every person has what they believe to be their purpose and objective in life. For instance, your current purpose and objective might be to be the best mother to your child. Maybe you are set on accomplishing various milestones as an employee and getting ahead in your career. Your objective could be simply to be as happy and satisfied as is humanly possible. The most important thing to do is to be clear on what this very essential need is in your life. Remember you are allowed to have multiple needs and categorize all of them as a priority. Now the next thing after identifying your needs is to determine the things that you require in order to meet these needs. For instance, a mother who wants to do the best by their child might require a supportive partner in order to be able to balance the demands of parenting and having a career. Such a mom will be uncompromising in their choice of partner. They will not allow a partner that is non-supportive and energy-sapping anywhere near them. This is because they have already defined and have a clear picture of what their needs are.

This type of mindset can also apply to the workplace. If you haven't determined what you need and what you won't stand for, you will often find yourself surrounded by the same energy vampires that you're trying your best to avoid. Defining your needs as an employee will help you determine what company to work for in terms of company culture, career progression, and compensation needs among others. A common problem that empaths have is not knowing when to speak up. As long as you know what your needs are, you will be in a position to speak up. When you are pushed to the wall you will be very clear about what is happening and take steps to change the situation because you are already familiar with your needs.

Take out a notebook right now and make a list of the things that you want from life. Take time to search your soul and figure out exactly what you would want from life if it was up to you. Now take a step back and realize that it is all up to you. Only you can determine what you get from life depending on the things you allow to happen. Use your notebook of needs and desires to remind yourself of what you are hoping to get out of life every time you start to feel muddled or depleted. If someone is responsible for making you feel muddled or depleted, remind yourself that this person is not acting in the best interest of your needs and then remove them from your life.

Stamp Boundaries in Your Life

In the beginning, empaths are known to have very weak boundaries and is something the empath must consciously work on to improve. Defining your needs will bring you to the very crucial second step of stamping boundaries and limits. Stamping boundaries in your life allows others to recognize what you will tolerate and what you won't tolerate. When you have boundaries, you teach other people how to treat you.

Many of the people that you initially meet do not know how to treat you and rely on the cues you give them to make sense of for themselves. Sure enough, there are some written common decency rules that govern social interactions. For instance, it is rude to ask out a woman when she is out and about with her husband. Almost everybody knows this. Those who do not yet know this will soon find out and in a very unpleasant manner. However, there are other personal rules that you might have that people do not know of. Let's say for instance that you have set aside an hour before bedtime to meditate. The colleagues you work with do not know this, so they keep calling you long after you've left the office to discuss work. Some of them call while you are in the middle of meditation. Meditation is your safe place and your time to recharge. Instead of being upset about your colleagues calling and keeping quiet about it, setting boundaries would look like this: Your colleague calls right before bedtime, you refuse to pick the call. The next morning you let them politely know that your evenings are set aside for family time and personal time. Chances are that they will not be calling you after work anymore.

Boundaries do not just apply to colleagues. You have to set

boundaries with your family and friends too. While most of us love our friends and families, it is important to recognize that they can also be very draining in their demands. When faced with an empath, some friends and family can take and take until there's nothing left to take. As an empath, you need to recognize that you can love someone and still say "no" to them if saying "yes" would be detrimental to you. Whether we are talking about saying yes every time a family member needs someone to babysit or saying yes to requests for funds and soft loans, you must be careful to draw the boundaries where they belong. After a while, people will realize that there are things that you will not allow in your life and will stop asking for favors at every turn. By doing this, you will be able to live a much happier life as you are in control of how you want to live your life and not letting others control you.

Take Note of the Energy Drainers and Energizers

In order to favorably impose your boundaries and limits, it will be essential to define the energy drainers and energizers in your life. Just as there are energy vampires that take away from you, there are people and situations that serve to boost your energy and morale. As a sensitive person, your energizers are assets that must be guarded. Long walks, alone time, communing with nature, and quality time spent with someone who truly loves you are all examples of energizers that an empath will benefit from. Once you know what steals your joy and what adds to it, you will be able to draw the lines regarding where each of them fits in your life.

Balance Your Chakras

Do you know what chakras are? According to Indian spiritual

thought, chakras are the energy points that every human being is born with. Every person has a total of seven chakras, which begin right at the start of the spine and go all the way up to the top of the head. The seven chakras are responsible for reenergizing you in various aspects of your life. For instance, the solar plexus chakra, also known as Manipura, is what gives you your self-identity and confidence. If your solar plexus chakra is underactive, you will struggle to make sense of who you are and even lack in self-esteem. If it is overactive, you might end up being egotistical or arrogant. Whether you ascribe to these beliefs or not, it is important to acknowledge that the premise of the chakras is one that makes total sense. As human beings, we are not just empty vessels that come to be and then complete our journeys in mortality. There is a driving force behind our actions and our lives. As an empath, it is important to ensure that you balance your chakras (or whatever you may prefer to call them) so that you can have a balanced life.

There are several simple tips that you can apply in your life to ensure that you awaken your chakras to help you be the best version of yourself. Walking barefoot, for instance, is known to connect you with the earth in what is known as grounding. In spiritual circles, grounding is the connection that happens between yourself as a spiritual person and the earth with all its energy. Grounding allows you to release all the bad energy that is pent up inside of you while getting some good energy from the earth in return. The chakra responsible for keeping you grounded to the energy of the earth is known as the root chakra. Grounding is vital for empaths who find themselves stuck in their head too much overthinking and overanalyzing.

Getting a relaxing massage and dancing are other ways you can fire up your chakras and heal yourself if you have been feeling a bit overwhelmed. If you do not have the time or opportunity for either, soak yourself in a warm bath complete with bath salts.

Epsom salts combined with lavender oil make for a very relaxing and energizing bath that will have you feeling reborn and completely balanced. While you are soaking in your bath, call positive thoughts into your mind by repeating affirmations such as *I am loved, I am safe, I am strong*.

Strengthen Your Mind with Positive Affirmations

Speaking of affirmations, that's another thing that you will need to learn as a long-term strategy if you wish to take control of your life as an empath. Positive affirmations serve to reinforce the empath's subconscious mind of who they truly are, what they believe and how they want to live their life.

For every one, as a young child, the subconscious mind is like a sponge. No matter what is in the environment, positive or negative, favorable or unfavorable, the sub-conscious mind will absorb it. So whatever negative traits and beliefs your parents have, it is most likely you picked up these unwanted traits and beliefs. And for the sensitive empath, the chances of absorbing these unfavorable beliefs and traits are much higher.

This is why self-awareness is so important, because we are able to observe the unwanted and make a conscious effort to remove this and reprogram our subconscious mind. Through the use of repetitive positive affirmations over a long period of time we are able to rewire the subconscious mind to create a much more desirable life, and can then help others to do the same.

Positive affirmations can be anything that you want them to be, as long as they are positive and encourage you to be your best self.

Example of positive affirmations that you can work with

include:

I am an empowered empath.

I am a calm and peaceful person.

I am smart and make sensible decisions.

I have the strength and wisdom to change my life.

I am not a prisoner of my mistakes.

I attract wealth and abundance into my life.

I surround myself with positive and uplifting energy.

Another thing to note with positive affirmations is that you can also use them to bring something into your life that you do not currently have but want to bring to your life. However, when you affirm this desirable thing, you must bring it into the present moment by speaking as if you already have it.

You do not want to affirm "I want." By affirming "I want" you are emitting the vibration "I want" and are only going to receive back the vibration of "I want" therefore, you will never truly manifest this desire. By emitting the vibration "I am" or "I have" that is the vibration you will receive and ultimately how you manifest what you truly desire, by affirming as if you already have it.

For example, let's say you desire a black Range Rover.

You would affirm: "I drive a beautiful black Range Rover." And as you affirm this desire, use the power of visualization and truly feel yourself gripping the steering wheel of the Black Range Rover with the brown leather interior driving down the road. Feel yourself in the moment.

A great example of a positive manifestation is Jim Carey writing himself a check for 10 million dollars to himself dated 10 years into the future, keeping it in his wallet. And after almost 10 years was up, he discovered that he was going to earn 10 million dollars for acting in the movie Dumb and Dumber. Amazing!

Make a list of the things that you want to affirm and attract right now and then use them as your affirmations to strengthen your mind and your reality. I would recommend then getting yourself an affirmation journal, so you have something organized to write down and store all your affirmations. You can go through your affirmations either first thing in the morning or right before you go to bed.

Express Gratitude

What would be a great addition right next to your affirmation journal is a gratitude journal. Affirmations and expressing gratitude tie in very well together and I recommend filling out both journals together. Let me explain why.

While you are a person that carries an impressive and admirable ability to detect other people's pain and bring them healing, you must always remember that you are the vessel through which the power of the universe flows. Remaining humble in the face of the gift that you have been bestowed with is a great way of ensuring that this gift continues to flourish. Arrogance has been known to stand in the way of many success stories. Do not let yours be one of them. Always take a few minutes of your time every day to express gratitude for what you are capable of doing. Expressing gratitude in your life serves two purposes. One is that it helps you to start seeing your ability as the gift that it is, and not as a burden that you have been yoked with. The second purpose gratitude serves is that when you vibrate on the frequency of gratitude, you will receive more things in your life to be grateful for, as that is the vibration you are emitting.

Here are some examples of gratitude statements to get your mind ticking:

I am grateful for the existence and experience of life.

I am grateful for my health.

I am grateful for my friends and family.

I am grateful for my shelter, clothing, food, and water.

I am grateful for the internet and being able to connect with my friend across the world.

I am grateful for my beautiful pets. They bring me so much joy to my life.

Can you already see the power of practicing gratitude? After hearing these statements of gratitude your mind already starts to feel more positive and you start to feel good about yourself. So many people complain and focus on what they DO NOT have and continue to vibrate on the frequency of lack! And what do you think they continue to receive...? More Lack!

Gratitude is extremely powerful and highly recommend your practice it if you want to change your life in a positive way.

Just like the affirmation journal, I would suggest investing in a gratitude journal, so you have something neat and organized to fill out daily, either first thing in the morning or just before you go to sleep. This will keep you accountable and you will be able to reflect back in time and notice the changes this simple activity has had on your life.

Listen to your Body!

It is not difficult for an Empath to be in tune with their body. They know when a meal makes them feel good and they know when a meal makes them feel ill. The problem is when you choose to ignore this feeling. Despite being able to be in tune with their body if they want to, empaths are susceptible to using food as an escape from their stressful life. However, doing this for a long period of time will only lead to shame and guilt so it is important to stay in tune with your body and only eat what makes you feel good after. Yes, the oily Chinese meal may taste good at the time, but you know immediately after you're going to feel like crap after and regret it.

If you are always eating fast food, you will have a harder time getting in touch with your inner and best self compared to someone who chooses to eat a well-balanced diet of protein, low-GI carbohydrates, and healthy fats. Respect all three macronutrients as each plays an important role in serving the body.

Additionally, make sure you get plenty of water to drink. Water flushes out toxins from the body and leaves you feeling hydrated and refreshed. The benefits of water can even be seen on the skin. You can go from breakout-prone skin to glowing skin in a matter of weeks if you keep up your water intake. If water can do such wonders to the skin (which is visible for all to see), imagine what it does on the inside. Water cleanses you from the inside out. It is no wonder that most empaths love water. Whether they are drinking it, swimming in it or taking a bath, most empaths swear by the cleansing and healing powers of water.

Meditation and Yoga

Pencil in meditation in your schedule and you will begin to notice yourself becoming more aware of your emotional and mental states. Meditation helps you to get rid of the clutter in your life while channeling in the good energy and focusing on the positive. A great thing about meditation is that there are numerous resources that are available on the Internet at no cost that can help you get better at meditating. You may choose to access YouTube channels that are dedicated to meditation or even download meditation apps from the app stores. Whichever way you go about it, you will soon notice that you will have an increased boost of energy and will feel calmer, more relaxed, and less irritable.

Yoga also serves a somewhat similar purpose. Having been in existence for over five thousand years, Yoga has been used mainly as a way of connecting to the higher power of the Universe. The original purpose of Yoga was to promote self-awareness and discernment in individuals and make them see where they stood in the overall big picture of the Universe.

Create Your Safe Place

This is probably the most important strategy the empath can implement in their life. Every empath requires a place that is free from the everyday distractions where they can retreat and recharge at the end of the day and be alone with their thoughts. It is important that you create a physical space where you feel absolutely safe and where you do not have to interact with anybody that you don't want to. Your safe place could be your own bedroom or even a restaurant that has a corner booth where you can hide away from everybody else. While in your safe place, make sure you switch off your cell phone and your mind as well so that the worries of the external world do not interrupt your moment of relaxation. Bring a notepad and pen with you and write down your thoughts, ideas, goals, and ambitions.

Chapter 6: Owning Your Superpowers

Being an empath does not have to be a fight against constant suffering and emotional drain. As an empath, you have a powerful gift that you can harness to make the world a better place. The ability to sense energy is not something that everyone has. As a matter of fact, research has shown that only approximately 20% of the world are labeled as highly sensitive, a label under which empaths loosely fall.

Furthermore, approximately 3% of the entire population qualifies as having a psychic empathic ability. What this means is that you are a minority in the world, but you can still use your talents to impact the rest of the world in a big way. Sometimes you do a lot just by focusing on those closest to you. Someone smart once said; be the change you wish to see in the world. As you make the conscious effort to work on your weaknesses and become the best version of yourself, you unconsciously give others permission to do the same.

Top Superpowers of Every Psychic Empath

You are probably wondering whether the only thing you will ever be good at is sensing emotion and feeling the pain of others. On the surface, it can seem as if this is all there is to a psychic empath. Fortunately, this is not the case. Empaths are gifted with great superpowers that they can use to do good in the world. If this comes as a surprise to you, then it is probably because you have been riddled with self-doubt unable to notice the amazing sides to your gift. Let's explore the superpowers of the psychic empath.

The Superpower of Vision and Discernment

When a psychic empath settles their mind and learns to work through the clutter of their everyday life, they can achieve a vision that normal people are not capable of. This is because such an empath is able to sift through the chaff and pick out the important details. Empaths have a three-sixty degree view on things, and for this reason, they can make extraordinarily visionary and discerning leaders. Of course, such an empath will also have to work through their typical lack of enthusiasm for leadership roles. When a willing empath takes on a leadership role, there is often a change for the better. They can read the people that they are leading well, anticipate their needs and put in place measures to cater for these needs. Because they are excellent listeners, empaths make people feel heard and listened to, which is a key quality of an exemplary leader.

The Superpower of Advanced Intuition

While other people struggle to hear their gut instinct clearly, the empath's intuition leaves nothing to chance; it is loud, clear and demands to be heard. In many cases, the only reason why an empath might fail to side with their intuition is because they chose to ignore it, not because it did not show up when required. A psychic empath's intuition is like a well-trained army with red flags that are hoisted every time there is approaching danger. This army works tirelessly and nonstop. A psychic empath that allows their army to flourish will easily tell you that your new partner is no good for you, even when you think you are head over heels in love with this person. Just by looking at a person, an empath can tell when that person has good intentions or otherwise. Empaths who trust their advanced intuition are able to avoid a whole lot of dangerous situations.

Additionally, the psychic empath can also use their advanced intuition when it comes to making tough decisions. They are able to use this gift to vividly sift through the array of options that are presented to them and ultimately determine which particular option resonates with them best.

The Superpower of Psychic Ability

Seeing that this book is called *Psychic Empath Warrior*, it would be improper for the empath's superpower of psychic ability to be missing from this list. The empath's psychic ability allows them to see things before they happen or even when they are happening even though they can be separated by thousands of miles from the actual event. An empath's psychic ability will allow them to feel the pain of a loved one who is undergoing a hurtful situation thousands of miles away. Have you ever caught yourself thinking about someone out of the blue and when you call them, they let you know that they were going through a tough time? This could be because of your psychic ability. Your nature as an empath will keep you connected to this person who is continents away, while your psychic ability enables you to receive signals, in the same way, that a distraught person might send SOS messages in the hope of being rescued. Further down in this chapter, there is a detailed exploration of the things that you can incorporate in your daily life to develop your psychic ability and make it better than it already is.

The Superpower of Healing

Whether they are healing by speaking life into others or just by surrounding others by their calm presence, empaths have quite an impact when it comes to alleviating the suffering of others. As an empath who has learned to steady themselves, your mere presence can be a healing balm to others. You only need to show up, and everyone else feels at ease. You probably know one or two of such people in your life. Their presence makes you feel safe and comfortable as if everything in the universe is aligned as it should be. If you do not know anybody like that, it just might be that you are that person. You might unknowingly be the calming presence in people's lives. What a great superpower to have, to be able to meet with a friend for coffee, fully understand the problem they are experiencing, and offer them helpful solutions. Of course, the important thing to remember with this superpower is that you must heal yourself first. You cannot fix other people's wounds when yours are bleeding.

The Superpower of Creativity

Empaths are highly talented and creative. It only makes sense—you cannot be so highly gifted and fail to make something out of it. Many empaths go on to create music that lasts generations, make art that wows the entire world for years, or write novels that captivate millions of people. It is rare to find an empath who does not have a creative bone in their body. Creativity is the empath's outlet. Creativity is the empath's chance to pour their souls out without being judged for it. Think about it: the empath who has had to battle their emotions, otherwise referred to as demons, all their life often needs a safe space where he or she can express exactly what they feel. This empath will turn to a platform such as painting, singing, exercising, drawing, film-making, writing and any other creative outlet that allows for freedom of expression. It is no wonder that a lot of creatives come up with concepts that have everyone else wondering why nobody thought of that before. It is simply because the mind of an empath is like a never-ending maze with surprises at every corner. The well of creativity that an empath embodies can never run dry. And the best part is that the empath feels their art. The art comes from deep down within them, and at the same time mirrors the emotions of the people around them because the empath is able to be selfless in their art.

Using Your Superpowers to Impact the World

When used correctly, the superpowers of an empath have the ability to change lives. Whether at work or in personal relationships, an empath's intuitive capability is their greatest asset. As an empath, you have something that many people struggle to have: the ability to read a situation instantly without needing to ask questions. Coupled with the superpowers discussed before, it's easy to see that empaths have a lot of potential to impact people and communities everywhere they go. The obvious question, therefore, becomes, how does an empath go about the process of channeling their superpowers towards the right causes? In other words, how can you take advantage of what you have to improve your life and those of others?

Creative Direction

Because of their highly intuitive nature, empaths often come in handy when it comes to offering creative direction in work projects and even in their own lives. Creativity is never usually the direct result of pure logic. For art to appeal to its audience, there has to be an element of intuitiveness and heartfelt emotion. That is why some of the most celebrated authors of all time are usually those who write with a lot of sadness. They are able to draw emotions from their readers because they feel and understand these emotions.

Ernest Hemingway, a world-famous American journalist and writer, once put it aptly this way: *"There's nothing to writing. All you do is sit down at a typewriter and bleed."* In this statement,

Hemingway was recognizing the thankless labor that is writing and at the same time appreciating that the magic of art cannot exist without feeling or emotion.

As an empath working in the creative industry, you should never shy away from sharing your opinions and views on projects. Some of them might seem outlandish or ridiculous but it is often the bold empath who is willing to wear their creative heart on their sleeve that wins the day and inspires others.

Nurturing Relationships

Psychic empaths make terrific friends. They are excellent listeners. They are empathetic. They anticipate other people's needs. They are often nurturing and rarely judgmental. One psychic empath friend is worth ten in the bush, so to speak. When a psychic empath meets a well-meaning person with whom they are able to nurture a respectful and mutually beneficial relationship, their friendship blossoms for years and years. It is indeed a thing to be proud of if you are an empath because you can be such a great friend to the people who need you.

Empaths are not just nurturing to their friends. They extend this trait to their colleagues as well. Work environments can often be ridden with anxiety and other forms of toxicity. For someone who is not attuned to or who is unable to understand this negative energy, such work environments can be very distressing. Empaths can filter through different types of energy and obtain important insights which allow them to navigate any environment mindfully. As such, empaths are likely to make thoughtful colleagues who think before they leap and who try to understand where others are coming before judging harshly.

Besides friendships and work relationships, empaths also thrive as parents. Empath parents often have so much positive energy, encouragement, and empowerment to pour into their children. After all, an empath understands what ails their child even when the child isn't in a position to articulate it. As an empath, whether you choose to have biological kids or adopt kids who need a home, there is a strong chance that you'll be one of those parents who grow up to become best friends with their children.

Mediation Roles

Because they are able to understand people without requiring words to be said, empaths often make great mediators in conflict resolution. Their ability to detect problems before they escalate into bigger issues allows the empath to be one step ahead in times of conflict. At the same time, they are also able to dig deep into a person's psyche and understand their greatest needs and wants, and thus realign the mediation exercise to do the same thing, which ensures that all parties feel like they've been listened to.

Activists and Advocates

As an empath, you have the potential to advocate for the unseen and the unheard because you are able to see and hear them. An empath's deep connection with their surrounding enables them to have a heightened understanding of issues. While some people will litter and shrug it off, an empath will find it highly disconcerting to go about life with such an obvious disregard for others and especially for the environment. It is, therefore, not uncommon to find many empaths involving themselves in advocacy roles such as fighting against environmental pollution, being activists for human and animal rights, and even helping to bring the marginalized to the forefront. In the eyes of the empath, social injustices cannot and must never be ignored.

What's even better is that empaths are able to connect easily with people, and thus influencing people to join worthy causes comes naturally to them. When an empath pleads their case, it's almost impossible to ignore.

Career Choices

The best careers for empaths are those that allow them to live out their full potential as healers and caregivers without burdening them unfairly with emotional and mental drain. If an empath decides to go down a more draining path, but still feels fulfilled in doing what they do, it's important for them to learn how to take care of themselves so they are not worn out on a constant basis. In careers where an empath is constantly exposed to the suffering of others or high levels of drama and negativity, it's highly crucial that the empath develops healthy coping and protecting mechanisms to avoid emotional drain.

There are certain careers that are better suited for empaths for several reasons. Empaths, for instance, make very good artists. As mentioned earlier, they are able to feel deeply and this gives them a creative edge over everyone else. A wise person once said that life imitates art. By choosing to become an artist, an empath is essentially lighting a torch to show the rest of the world how to live. A great advantage of being an artist is that you don't even need to show your face to the rest of the world. You can allow your art to communicate on your behalf while protecting yourself from public attention, which can often be overwhelming. An artist who has chosen this approach is Banksy. Banksy, now 45-years old and based in England, has managed to influence the world with his art while maintaining his anonymity. His debut as a street artist was back in the 1990s and to date, nobody has been able to unveil his real identity.

Freelance writing and travel blogging are two other career choices that are ideal for the empath who wants to explore their creative side, impact people, move freely, and recharge their minds and bodies while keeping human interaction to a minimum. To be clear, this isn't to say that empaths hate working with people. Rather, empaths thrive more and make better use of their superpowers when they work in environments that allow their vulnerable sides to flourish without negative energy.

As an empath, you may also consider becoming an online coach or therapist. In both cases, you will be helping others and because there are guidelines to the kind of care you need to provide, you are able to help others while also safeguarding yourself. Other examples of safe and fulfilling career routes for empaths include charity, social work, and healthcare, especially mental healthcare. Empaths also make great veterinarians since they are able to deeply care for animals.

Overall, empaths do well in self-employment and in professions where they are able to help others. When an empath is in a profession that is a perfect match for their personality, they leave a tremendous impact that resonates with everyone they come into contact with.

As an empath, you may have previously struggled with holding down a job. It is important to recognize that this may be because you had chosen the wrong kind of job, or intuitively, your soul was trying to tell you that there is something else out there much better suited you. Something your soul is craving to express. With the right career, you can change lives.

Another path to consider as an empath is an entrepreneurship. This may sound daunting at first but let's break it down on why this is a good idea. Being an entrepreneur provides a great sense of freedom, which all empaths love. You set your own rules and your own work schedule. You are not bound by the limitations of having a boss. You do not need to ask for permission when to take a vacation or when to go to the bathroom. Additionally, in the field of entrepreneurship, you must know what the market wants. You must be able to provide to the market with something they are happy with. Something that is going to solve their problem. This is where the empath is truly able to shine. Using their ultimate gift of empathy, they are able to truly dive into the mind of the market and truly understand their pains and problems. And with this, can deliver a product to the market that satisfies greatly. Entrepreneurship also acts as a medium where the empath can unleash their creativity and come up with ideas and solutions, bringing great joy to the empath.

The worst careers for empaths include those which require one to be aggressive and competitive, deal with crowds, interact with a lot of people, and play by rules which are sometimes unreasonable or even unscrupulous. Professions such a politics, sales, and public relations don't suit most empaths.

Detecting Manipulation

An empath's ability to sense a person's negative energy even when the person is trying to disguise it as something else allows them to tell when a person is lying, even though everyone else may be in the dark. An empath who has learned to understand other people's energies without getting drawn into them is able to sense subtle energy shifts which may point towards potential manipulation. Manipulators use the same book of tricks including using body language and eye contact to create rapport with the intent of creating an aura of harmlessness. For the inexperienced eye, this kind of rapport may come across as genuine. Fortunately for empaths, inauthenticity is often detected from a mile away.

This ability allows empaths to protect themselves and those around them from predators who may be looking to take advantage. Since time immemorial, children have been implored to listen to their mothers since "mothers know best." The reason for this is that mothers are highly intuitive towards their children and are therefore able to predict danger even before the children can sense it. That is why your well-meaning mother might take one look at a girlfriend or boyfriend that you have just introduced to her and tell you that you're about to get into trouble. This kind of sixth sense that mothers have towards their offspring is the same that empaths have towards most people and situations.

Diffusing Negative Energy

The energy of an empath is light and positive by nature. When they're overwhelmed by other people's negative energies, empaths tend to be the light in the darkness. Just by being present in a place, an empath can make people experience lightness and positivity that starkly contrasts the energy that is often emitted by predators.

Even if you're shy to talk to people and hate crowded settings, you can use your mere presence to make others feel better. Sometimes, words aren't even required. There is so much negative energy in the world that it makes all the difference if one person can be that lighthouse in the dark that shows those stranded in the dark sea that there is hope in the horizon.

Mistakes Stopping You from Exploring Your Superpowers

The unfortunate thing about the empath's superpowers is that they rarely get used. A lot of the time, empaths do not even realize that they are so incredibly gifted. And when they do, there are empaths who choose to have nothing to do with their superpowers. Why is this so? Why are many empaths afraid to unleash their full potential? There are several mistakes that are committed knowingly and unknowingly by an empath that stand in the way of their superpowers.

Wanting to Fit In

The desire to fit in causes many empaths to hide their powers behind curtains where nobody can find them. Truth be told, being an empath is not easy. You will not always feel normal. You might come off as a bit weird or even crazy. An empath who is aware of their power and realizes that they might be judged for it might choose to hide behind normal. You must remember that there is nothing interesting about normal. If you were meant to be normal, you would not have been gifted as you are. Different is good. Weird is good. You only need to learn how to embrace these weird parts of you. It is indeed true that nobody can make you feel inferior without your permission. If the world sees that you are comfortable in who you are, you can bet that there will not be many people calling you weird. And even if they do, the joke is on them because you have all these superpowers and they don't!

Thinking You're Too Much

You have grown up hearing the word *too emotional, too sensitive, too dramatic,* and t*oo much* used in relation to you and because of this you have decided that you are indeed too much to handle. If you show up in the world when you have already written yourself off, then the rest of the world will follow suit. You are not too much of anything. You are exactly what you were born to be. The shoes you wear are huge and not many people would dare to step in them. Embrace yourself for the masterpiece that you are, and instead of thinking that you are too much let those who are able to handle you stay in your life. Anybody else is welcome to leave just as they came. Remember that you have surmounted emotional labor that would easily break others. You fight emotional battles every day and come out unscarred. How dare you call yourself anything other than a hero!

Lacking Confidence

The way you speak, the way you walk, how you dress yourself up every morning before getting to work…these are things that can impact how good you feel about yourself, and how others perceive you. Of course, confidence is deeper than the Gucci belt on your waist, or the Ray-Ban designer sunglasses protecting your eyes as you sunbathe. Most empaths are introverts; introverts are not always known for speaking their minds. An empath might even choose to keep quiet for the sake of keeping the peace and avoiding confrontation. You've got to remember that the signals you send out into the world are the very same signals that the world will judge you by. If you come across as the shrinking violet, you will always and forever be that. However overwhelming you find crowds to be, you can still let your presence be known. A well-spoken and firmly articulate word in the middle of a meeting will allow you to share your creative self with your colleagues. It does not have to be a ten-minute explanation or justification that wears you down and gets you fighting negative energy from the opposing seniors. You only need to make sure that you believe in yourself, and that other people know that, and let them know that they have a reason to believe in you too. Most people have a way of taking advantage of the guy with no confidence—they make this person the doormat who is used and discarded at pleasure. Do not be this person.

Neglecting Physical Well-being

As an empath, it is typical to focus on getting the emotional bits healed while you neglect everything else. This makes sense seeing that emotions make up a huge part of the empath's life. However, it is important that you work on your physical body as well. Your mind will only work well when it is inside of a healthy body. Yoga, swimming, weight-lifting, and other low impact exercises can turn around your physical health and develop into a real passion that you can put energy into. You need to find a physical outlet for all the pent up tension and emotion in your body. What's more, physical exercise releases endorphins and dopamine, the feel-good hormones, which will have you feeling happier and refreshed in no time. If you do not believe that physical exercise does indeed make the empath happier, try one boxing class at your local gym. Imagining that the punching bag is your insufferable boss will have you rejoicing in the relief of revenge and you will not have to be so uptight around your boss next time they try to rile you. This does not mean that violence is ever the answer but every once in a while, you need to punch something that will not cry, if only to let out some of that steam that many empaths walk around with.

Forgetting to Laugh

Not everything needs to be serious in an empath's life. The emotional load that you carry is serious enough, so why burden yourself with the constant need to be serious? Learning to laugh at yourself is one of the greatest things that you can do for yourself. There will be days when your psychic ability will be off, and others when unusual coincidences will show up at your door. Take it all at your own stride. Being a psychic empath is not an excuse to go about life with a sour look on your face. You can be an empath and still have fun with it. Train yourself to see the funny side of everyday life and you will have the right kind of wrinkles. Laughter is referred to as the best medicine because of its ability to lift even the lowest of spirits. If you can find something to laugh about every day, then you will have moments in your day when you are not worried about other people's energy or emotions.

Refusing to Jump In

While the empath often encourages others to go in the direction of their dreams, the same does not apply to self-talk. Many empaths will spend hours analyzing why they need to be doing one thing and not the other. This is how the empath misses out on the best adventures of their life as they overthink. If your intuition has given you the green light to proceed with something, do not hesitate. Do it. You do not have to mull over the matter with your logical mind. If you do so you will only find yourself in an inescapable rabbit hole that is full of excuses as to why you should not do a particular thing. At the end of the day, your story becomes full of what-ifs instead of one full of great memories. Learn to jump in and see what happens—whether it is a relationship, a career, moving to a new place. The worst thing that can happen is that you will not like it, which only means that you will have to reconsider but at least you will have tried and gained new knowledge.

Fine Tuning Your Psychic Abilities

So far, the bulk of this book has been about getting you in the right mental and emotional frame to be the best version of your psychic empath self. Being right in your mind and in your emotions is the starting point to success in life, whether you are talking about being good at psychic empathy or anything else under the sun. You can only do right in the world if you do right by yourself. Now, after getting yourself well-grounded and self-aware of your abilities you might begin to wonder how you can be better at who you are. After all, aren't some psychic empaths so good at what they do that they become national heroes who go on to change the world? Wouldn't you want to be such a great empath that you are called upon to impact the world in a positive way? While not every psychic gets to reach the pinnacle of their paranormal ability, you are capable of developing your psychic abilities to get better at who you are.

Journal

While in the process of walking through the somewhat confusing maze that is the life of a psychic empath, you will accumulate lots of information that you need to process through. This information may be collected through conversations that you have with others or even via dreams. Either way, you will need to keep track of these little bits of information and in a way that does not clutter your mind. The best way to do this is by keeping a journal. If you had a strange dream about someone, write this down in your journal. You will have a detailed account to refer to when the events of the dream come to play out in real life. Journaling will also help you identify patterns of your psychic ability. Perhaps you will notice that you tend to have these strange dreams after talking to a particular person or visiting a specific place.

Befriend Other Psychic Empaths

One problem associated with being a psychic empath is that there is no professional organization of psychic empaths that meet once every year for networking purposes. It is common to feel alone and isolated as a psychic empath, but the good news is that you have kindred spirits in the world. You only need to know where to find them. A psychic empath who spends his or her days worn out by the energy of people around them will do well to surround themselves with people who understand exactly what they go through. A good place to get started on your search for kindred spirits is at your local spirituality classes. If there are no classes near where you live, you can still look up spiritual development circles and events in your region. Packing your bags and retreating to the mountains for a week of spiritual healing, awakening, and connection is worth the several months of clarity and fortitude that you will have after interacting with people who are like you. You may also come out of such events with lifelong friends and even mentors.

If you are still not able to find any sort of groups around your region there are plenty of Facebook Groups for empaths that offer tremendous amounts of value and help.

Develop Your On and Off Switch

One of the things you'll quickly appreciate as your psychic abilities develop is your control over them. It is important that you remain in control of your abilities so that they do not rule over your life. Having an on and off switch, so to speak, is important in ensuring that you are not in psychic mode at all times. You can develop your on and off switch by visualizing something that you need to do before and after engaging your psychic abilities. It could be something as simple as imagining yourself walking down a hallway and pushing a door open and then closing it afterward when you are done.

Maintain a High Vibration

Everything on earth has its own energy and from this energy comes the vibration. Your vibration changes depending on your thoughts and moods. A person that is negative, jealous, and critical will have dense energy that vibrates lowly. A cheerful and positive person, on the other hand, will have light energy that vibrates fast, thus drawing positive people to them. When people say that they do not like the vibe that a certain person gives off, it is correct to take this literally. Some people just have bad vibes, while others have good ones. Low vibration brought on by dark energy will attract its own kind, while high vibration will do the same. If you wish to tune into your psychic abilities, you will need to ensure that you are vibrating at higher frequencies than the average person. What you have is a special gift and you cannot afford to vibrate like the common person in the street. To attract the high energy that will help you become better at being psychic, you must be willing to emit this energy.

There are several things you can do to ensure that you set your vibration at a higher frequency than everybody else. To start with, you can simply train your mind to be more positive and to see the good side of everything so that you are not constantly weighed down by dark thoughts. Being out in nature and opening your heart to love is another way of ensuring you are always carrying the good energy that you need and deserve. Children and pets are especially great at giving the unadulterated kind of love that every psychic empath could benefit from. If you have a pet, spend a few moments every day where you just cuddle them and enjoy the closeness of this beautiful creature that loves you without demanding anything in return. This is going to perk your spirits right up, and high spirits equal high vibrations.

Watch what you eat as well. If you are always binging on high-sugar and high-carb processed foods, you will likely find yourself lacking in the good energy that comes from wholesome foods. Fruits and vegetables are especially great foods that will help you stock up on the good energy that you need. Fruits and vegetables absorb energy from the sun and transfer this energy to us when we eat them.

If you have always enjoyed getting a natural tan, now you have another reason why basking in the sun is even more important. It is not for no reason that the sun remains a revered source of energy, dating as far back as ancient cultures. The goodness of the sun goes beyond warming our skins and giving us important vitamins for bone development. Absorbing some of the sun's goodness is bound to leave you feeling energized and ready to vibrate on a higher frequency. Make sure that you protect yourself by not staying in the sun for too long as you do not want to burn your skin.

Silence the Noise

Your sixth sense is strongest when your mind is quiet and peaceful. The proverbial voice in your head that stops you from making stupid decisions is often your third eye trying to show you that the path you're taking is dangerous. Unfortunately, while being persistent in its means to communicate awareness, your sixth sense is also very measured in its tone. In the presence of noise and clutter, you'll not be able to hear a thing. So, learn how to cultivate silence in order to give your sixth sense a chance to be heard. Whether you're meditating, taking a walk or enjoying a lap or two in the swimming pool, train your mind to be quiet. Pause and take a breath and only then will you be able to hear the whispers of your sixth sense.

Cultivate Creativity

The rational mind is an enemy of the third eye. The rational mind often defeats the sixth sense with logic. Rationalizing things is often what causes people to make bad decisions even when their sixth sense is screaming for them to stop. To combat this problem, consider nurturing your creative side. In creativity, your imaginative side takes over from your rational side. Creativity doesn't require you to be perfect or logical. In a pottery class, there are no marks for perfect pots. Rather, such a class is an opportunity for you to let loose and allow your mind to be free and uninhibited. Other alternatives could be learning how to play an instrument or how to salsa dance. Once you take over the reins from the logical mind, you can allow your sixth sense to roam free because then the possibilities become endless.

Use All Senses Together

You don't want to become over-reliant on your sixth sense, as this could interfere with your decision-making processes and make you a tad bit paranoid. When overused, the sixth sense can be worn down. The important thing is to maintain a healthy balance between your third eye and all your other senses. This way, you filter your perception through different channels and arrive at the most informed conclusion.

Third Eye Chakra Cleansing

Chapter 5 introduces the concepts of chakras and their place in the empath's world. Feel free to go back to this chapter if you need some refreshing.

The third eye, otherwise known as the mind's eye or the sixth chakra, is thought to be an invisible eye that gives one a more heightened perception of things. In other words, the third eye is the well from which your sixth sense springs. In graphical illustrations, the third eye is usually shown to be located at the center of your forehead. When it comes to the third eye, there are three categories of empaths. The first category includes empaths who don't know of the third eye's existence, while the second category is made up of those who know it exists and use it sparingly, almost as if they are afraid of unleashing its full potential. The final category is made up of empaths who have embraced the full glory of the third eye and use its power and perception to direct their everyday decisions. Ideally, all empaths should open their third eye, which in this case means honing your sixth sense so that you can see what is beyond the ordinary.

There are many breathing and visualization exercises that are thought to unblock the third eye chakra. Engaging in such exercises prepares your third eye to be in an optimum state to detect and send out perceptions.

Here is a mini exercise:

1. First, you'll need to ensure that you are in a relaxed state, whether lying down or seated upright in a quiet room.

2. Slowly breath in and out deeply and repeat this ten times.

3. As you inhale and exhale, imagine a purple ball of light straight at the middle of your forehead where your third eye is said to be located.

4. Imagine that the ball of light is collecting all the negative thoughts from your mind, with the intention of purging them. The more the ball of light grows, the more negative energy it purges.

5. Imagine yourself taking in the positive energy of your newly-cleansed third eye.

6. Repeat this exercise until you're certain that all the blockages of your third eye have been eliminated.

Be sure to do some further research into the third eye as it will provide great benefits for you. The reason why it's important to ensure the third eye is clear and working as designed is because if this isn't the case, an empath is likely to feel indecisive, overwhelmed, paranoid, hopeless, and maybe even insignificant and lacking in purpose. A fully functional third eye allows the empath to see beyond the minor details and focus on the bigger picture instead.

Embody Compassion in Your Everyday Life

Do not be so focused on honing your psychic abilities that you forget to live in your present and natural world where there are people that need your love and compassion. It might be exciting to live in a world that nobody else can see but you also run the risk of pushing away the people around you. Practice compassion in your everyday life and you will soon see some of it come back to you. When this happens, you will find yourself surrounded by positive energy, which will put you in an even better place to develop your abilities. Above all else, practice compassion for the simple reason that there are people who could really use it. The selfless compassion of a psychic empath is the never-ending well that nourishes others while feeding the empath as well.

Refuse to Tolerate Negative Energy

While practicing compassion in your daily life is a great act, it is important to realize that you will still come across negative people from time to time. If you grew up in a violent or negative household it is likely you have grown used to this sort of behavior and treatment. But this does not have to be your default anymore. You have a choice.

The old you may have tolerated and just 'dealt' with someone who likes to constantly complain and cause drama, or even worse, put you down, but the new empowered version of yourself must refuse to tolerate negative energy and negative people. Say 'no' and walk away. Respect yourself and love yourself.

Energy is contagious and therefore it is important to surround yourself with positive, uplifting, and inspiring energy. And by doing so, you will allow yourself to live a happier life and grow yourself and your abilities much higher providing greater internal fulfillment.

Build a Healthy and High Sense of Self-Worth

This is something that is not changed overnight but nonetheless a vital and healthy focus to have in order to become an empowered psychic empath warrior. There is no one particular step to increase your self-worth to a healthy and high level but rather a combination of many pieces of the puzzle. As you combine everything we have talked about so far, you unapologetically allow yourself to shine to the highest level and truly become a positive impact on the world providing massive value to people who also want to become better versions of themselves.

Chapter 7: Common Myths That Psychic Empaths Should Never Believe

As if being highly sensitive to the energy around you is not already a big responsibility, you will also have to contend with a lot of misconceptions about you. As an empath, you really have a big calling on your hands and you need to understand that not everyone will understand this. You might be labeled as being too emotional or too dramatic. You might even be accused of being one of the energy vampires that you are so keen to eliminate from your life. Understanding the many misconceptions that people have in regard to empaths is the first step towards gently educating those around you. Even if you do not feel like being the myth buster in your circle, you can still learn to differentiate the myths from the facts for your own sake. Knowledge is power and having knowledge about yourself is one of the most powerful things you can do for yourself.

Myth #1: Psychic empaths are extremely self-absorbed and only worry about themselves.

Fact: Psychic empaths often care about others more than they care about themselves.

From the outside looking in, the moodiness and emotional nature of a psychic empath can come across as the disposition of a person who is only concerned with how they are feeling. The truth of the matter is that a psychic empath is more likely to be moody because of the people around them, and not because of their own emotions. It is easy to be judgmental towards a psychic empath because of how they carry themselves. They are often quiet and reserved and will not want to come out to play too often. This might be interpreted to mean that they do not care about interacting with others and only worry about themselves. The truth is that while the empath might want to be a ray of sunshine to everyone else, they often find themselves incapable because of the overwhelming feelings they go through when dealing with different energies given out by others.

Myth #2: Psychic empaths are just mentally ill.

Fact: Being highly sensitive is not a mental illness.

Many empaths make for good listeners and confidants based on their ability to empathize and truly feel for others. Because of this, empaths often find themselves the designated dumping ground for all emotional baggage. When you are burdened with the emotional problems of others, it is easy to become depressed and anxious, which might cause others to assume you are mentally ill. Many times, empaths are just sad because of all the emotional burden that they have to shoulder. This immense sadness may mimic the signs of a person that is going through clinical depression. Yes, there are instances when an empath may be diagnosed with depression, but this is not simply because they are highly sensitive. There are numerous factors that must be present for one to be diagnosed with depression. These factors are not exclusive to an empath. They can affect just about anyone, especially those who are genetically predisposed to the same.

Myth #3: Empaths are psychologically weak

Fact: The moments of "weakness" that empaths exhibit are as a result of all the negative energy that they have to deal with.

What might be normal to a typical non-empath may be extremely difficult to the empath. Take, for instance, holding down an office job. For the person that is not highly sensitive to the energy of other people, an office job is just another opportunity to earn a paycheck and advance in their career. For the empath, an office job means being constantly bombarded by the negative energy from all sides. As such, an empath might struggle to hold down a normal 9 to 5 job, while this is just another workday for everyone else. When this happens, the empath might be accused of being weak, lazy, fussy or just unwilling to try. This could not be further from the truth. Being an empath is hard work. Imagine walking through life everyday while someone carries a huge ball that they hit you with every time you take one step. This is how it feels to be an empath. You are constantly being hit by a big ball of negative energy and you must lift yourself up every time you fall from this hit. After a while, it can be easier to stay on the ground because you have run out of energy to lift yourself up. As an empath, it is important to remember that you are not psychologically frail. Being able to deal with other people's negative energy on a daily basis and showing up in the world even though you know what's coming, takes a whole lot of strength.

Myth #4: Empaths are emotionally volatile

Fact: Being exposed to varying emotional energy can make you more in control of your emotions.

People who believe that empaths are emotionally volatile base their arguments on the fact that empaths are often exposed to various energies, which might interfere with how emotionally stable they are. True, it is common for an empath to be moody, but this does not mean that they are always going to lash out when provoked. Many empaths are often moody when they retreat into themselves to introspect on the emotions that they have picked up. This does not make them a volatile person who is at the mercy of their emotions. It is possible for an empath to be highly stable when it comes to their feelings and those of others. In fact, an empath can easily learn how to be calm and in control regardless of those around them by understanding how to process and shield the energy that surrounds them. Some of the calmest and collected people that exist in this world are actually empaths. They have learned to read people and so nothing really takes them by surprise.

Myth #5: Most empaths are cold and detached from everyone else.

Fact: Detachment is a side effect of being emotionally drained.

As discussed in Chapter 3, it is possible for an empath to become detached over time if they have gone through tough periods of emotional drain. Many empaths who come across as detached do not become so because they intended to. It is often as a result of being emotionally abused by people around them. When they cannot take it anymore, an empath may become numb as a way of protecting themselves. It is not correct to assume that an empath is cold and unfeeling simply because they are an empath. Even the most outwardly detached empaths tend to have a light of empathy flickering deep inside of them. Empathy is not something you can switch on and off at will. If you care about other people, you will always care about them regardless of where you go or what you do.

Myth #6: Empaths are often highly dependent on their loved ones.

Fact: Empaths like for positive energy to flow both ways.

When an empath finds a source of positive energy, that source becomes an asset that they can draw their strength from. This is why empaths really thrive when they are deeply and genuinely loved. However, unlike energy vampires, empaths realize the need for the flow of positive energy to be two-sided. They love giving as much as they enjoy taking. You are not likely to find an empath that loves leeching on their loved ones. It is also important to note that empaths are not really dependent on positive energy from other people to survive. They are capable of doing it all on their own, as long as they learn how to protect from negative energy around them. If you are an empath, you do not have to worry about being a leech to others. As long as nobody is complaining, and as long as you can feel the good, positive energy flowing both ways, then it is safe to assume that the people in your life love you and the presence you bring.

Myth #7: Empaths are just glorified doormats.

Fact: With the right boundaries, an empath can care about others without feeling used.

Sure enough, empaths struggle with saying no. Empaths often want to take care of others and struggle with the guilt of feeling as if they are not helpful. It is effortless for an empath to find themselves relegated to the role of a doormat if they have not set the limits and boundaries for other people. This; however, does not mean that all sensitive people are just pushovers that allow anyone and everything in their lives. Empaths who are conscious of their powers and abilities know that it is easy for others to take advantage of them. As such, they often have ways of managing the people in their lives and striking the balance between being helpful and being everyone's doormat.

Myth #8: Empaths are all good people.

Fact: Being highly sensitive does not automatically qualify you for decency.

The question of whether a person is good or bad can only be answered after evaluating the choices that the person makes, and not as a factor of their genetic predisposition. Just because a person has been born as an empath does not mean they will always be a good person. An empath is a human being who is capable of hurting others and even making bad choices based on the prevailing circumstances in their life. While it is true that many empaths are often not manipulative people, it is also true that they are just humans and have the choice to be bad or good just like everyone else.

Myth #9: Empaths take to narcissists like moths to a light.

Fact: The relationship between empaths and narcissists is complex.

It has been said that opposites attract, and this could never be overstated in the case of narcissists and empaths. Empaths are the complete opposite of narcissists, and when these two categories of people meet there are often fireworks. Why is this so? Is it because the empath is keen on healing the narcissist? In many cases, the empath is not even aware that they are dealing with a narcissist. This might seem like a contradiction because after all, empaths are supposed to be intuitive and highly capable of reading other people's energy and intentions. Narcissism is a personality disorder that brings forth individuals who are highly manipulative. At the beginning of a relationship, the narcissist might make it seem as if they are the healer that the empath needs. As such, the empath will gravitate towards the narcissist because they seem kind and decent and loving. The narcissist, on the other hand, will pursue the empath because they love the adoration that the empath is able to give so freely. The narcissist-empath relationship evolves to become a highly toxic relationship where the empath keeps on giving and forgiving, while the narcissist cannot stop taking and creating chaos because that is what they thrive in. There is often never a happy ending when a narcissist and an empath meet and fall in love.

Myth #10: All empaths are introverted.

Fact: Empaths can be introverted, or not.

Empaths do not all come in one size. There are different sides to an empath. Some are introverted, some are extroverted, while some are ambiverts. In all fairness, the extroverted empath is rarer than the introverted empath. However, reliable sightings point to the existence of the paradox that is an empath who is extroverted. Being extroverted is more of a personality trait than anything else. As such, you can be a person that loves to be around people and at the same time be highly capable of tuning into the emotions of those people. An extroverted empath gets to live a very conflicting life in that they want to interact with people but at the same time, they do not want to be overwhelmed by it. This is unlike the case of the introverted empath who could not care much for crowds. If you are an extroverted empath, you will need to be careful about how much you take in from others before wearing yourself down. For every two or so hours spent in a crowd, make sure you take some time to catch your breath and process out the negative energy from your body.

Myth #11: You can quit being an empath.

Fact: Being an empath is a life-long sentence.

Many empaths would love to be able to wake up one day and find that their empathic abilities are all gone. It can be overwhelming to be the resident empath, and sometimes you will feel that you need a break from all the caring. Unfortunately, if you are born an empath there simply is no way out of it. Instead of fighting your power, the best thing you can do for yourself is to learn how to harness it for your own good, and for the good of those around you. For example, you can train yourself to learn how to distinguish your emotions from those of others so that you do not carry emotional loads that do not belong to you. You may not be able to stop being an empath, but you sure can learn how to carry this gift without breaking your back.

Myth #12: Empaths are victims of childhood trauma.

Fact: Trauma is not a prerequisite for empathy.

Some people believe that the only way a person can be as emotional as the empath typically is if that person has gone through some form of childhood trauma. It is wrong to assume that a person who is sensitive towards others and in regard to their own emotions is automatically coming from a place of great suffering. True, there are empaths who have suffered greatly at the hands of those who were supposed to love and protect them. However, it is inaccurate to think that the driving force behind empathy is trauma. Some people are simply born with the ability to be highly sensitive. What happens to them as they grow up is a whole different matter.

Conclusion

The life of a psychic empath is by no means easy, but the gift of psychic empathy is not a small one either. It has been said that great power comes with great responsibility. Such is the case of a psychic empath who has been gifted a rare ability to see into others. With this ability comes the need to ensure that the psychic empath remains fair to themselves while also impacting others positively with their gift. Psychic empaths struggle with this balance all their lives, especially because they are often dismissed as too emotional or too sensitive when they bring it up. This book is intended to ensure that you never have to conform to these labels because you will have known better by the time you get to the final chapter. With this book, you are now in a better position to articulate who you are and what you are capable of instead of simply worrying that you overreact to situations.

Hopefully, you have had your fair share of a-ha moments when reading this book while identifying the enemies in your life and understanding why you sometimes feel the way you do even though there seems to be no reasonable explanation for it. It is important to always keep in mind that as a psychic empath, your number one enemy is your mind and the things that you allow to go on in your mind. While energy vampires like narcissists and the like may attempt to suck the soul out of you, your mind is the real landmine. It is in your mind that you wallow in thoughts and emotions, overthinking and over-processing other people's feelings and moods. It is your mind that keeps you company when you retreat to the solitude of your alone time. It is your mind that can change whether you see your ability as a good thing or a thing that you wish you did not have.

Conquering your mind so that it works for you and not against you will be one of the bravest things that you do for yourself as a psychic empath. Chapter 4 and 5 are complete with practical suggestions of things that you can do to conquer your mind, one step at a time. These suggestions can be implemented on a short-term and long-term basis and have been grouped appropriately.

After conquering your mind, you will then be tasked with ensuring that you use your empathic abilities for good. This does not mean lying flat so that others can walk on you. It means that you will need to learn who can be helped and who will not benefit much from your concern. It's all a matter of balance.

Lastly, you must understand that you will have good days and bad days. As a psychic empath, there will be days when your mind will go on a thinking spree and emotions will overcome you. It is important to remember that before anything else, you are a human and you are allowed to experience the full extent of the human condition. You are allowed to have good days, bad days and everything in between. You are allowed to have days when you spend all your hours helping others, and the days when you lock yourself up in your house and binge-watch your favorite series. Just because you are a psychic empath does not mean that you are obliged to dedicate all your days to saving humanity. Save some for yourself. Be kind to yourself as you are to others. Enjoy the journey of exploring what adventures your gift will take you on. It is often in the most unexpected of moments that we stumble upon our true happiness. May you stumble upon your happiness as you heal yourself and others.

If you found this material anyway helpful and beneficial to you, please let me know in the form of a review. I would love to hear from you. It brings me great fulfillment to know that my work is able to help any of the lost souls out there.

Thank you.

Goodbye for now, psychic empath warrior.

www.ingramcontent.com/pod-product-compliance
Lightning Source LLC
Chambersburg PA
CBHW071010080526
44587CB00015B/2415